How to Win at Giving Presentations

Also by Mack Munro

How to Build Better Bosses

How to Be a Great Boss

How to Build a Culture of Engagement

How to Win at Performance Management

How to Win at Giving Presentations

By
Mack Munro

First Edition

KDP . Vanleer, TN

How to Win at Giving Presentations

Published by KDP

ISBN: 9781092604208

Printed in the United States of America

Quantity discounts are available on bulk purchases of this
book for educational training purposes, fund-raising, or gift
giving. For more information, contact us at the address
below. Special books, booklets, or book excerpts can also
be created to fit your specific needs. For more information,
contact Marketing Department, Main Line Press,
P.O. Box 75, Vanleer, TN 37181.

For all of those who would rather hold a snake, face a loaded gun, walk on hot coals in their bare feet, or hug their mother-in-law than give a presentation...

This book is for you!

"Do or do not. There is no 'try'"

Yoda

Table of Contents

*"Fear is like fire: If controlled, it will help you;
if uncontrolled, it will rise up and destroy you."*

John F. Milburn

About This Book

Before every presentation I give or workshop that I facilitate, I say a silent prayer that nobody shows up.

I know that sounds strange coming from a guy who's been teaching and speaking full time since 2004, but it's true. Speaking makes me nervous. Sometimes even afraid.

But that's normal. And, if you have to give a presentation or teach a class, you'll feel it too. The key is learning how to leverage that fear and transform it into energy. This book shows you how to do that.

Now about this book. Back in 2005, I wrote what I thought was the definitive guide to giving a great presentation. The book was titled: *Podium Paranoia – Transforming Fear into Knockout Presentations.* It took me over a year to write and I couldn't wait for it to launch.

But few people bought it. Very few. I was frustrated. I know for a fact that most people fear speaking in front of a group and would avoid it at all costs. Why then, with such a great resource available, would people not buy it?

I never found the answer so the book sat for a few years languishing on Amazon. It might still be out there. Who knows? But as I found out, who cares?

And so I went on doing workshops and building my business. Fast forward to now, my focus is on helping companies build better bosses and helping bosses do a better job. And in doing that, I found one area that bosses really suck at is in giving presentations. Not big keynotes like I do, but simple presentations, like safety briefs, stand-up meetings, and of course briefing executives. The more I saw this, the more I realized that the old dusty, moldy *Podium Paranoia* book had the answers. So I took out the manuscript and updated it.

Significantly as it turns out. After all, back in 2005, you were really cool if you used *PowerPoint*® but now it's an expectation. Back then, audiences weren't distracted by mobile devices, but they are now.

But just like then, information still needs to be passed along. If you're The Boss, you can't screw this up. And If I work for you, I hope you've got the courage to get up in front of the executives and communicate our issues to them. A Boss that can't do a presentation is useless.

Don't be useless! This book is designed for someone who is going to make a presentation in front of a large crowd but the techniques will work with small groups and even one-on-one. I break the topic down into small bites and give you lots of lists and checklists. The answers are all here for you, you just need to read them and put them into practice.

And that brings us to a final point before we jump into the material. You must practice! If you're afraid of speaking, the only way to cure it is to do it more often. Practice doesn't make perfect, but it does breed confidence. Shortly after I wrote this book back in 2005, I got a contract position teaching civilian transition skills to retiring and separating military members. This was a three-day program done in front of audiences between 50 and 80 people. Lectures, not really interactive sessions. I did this three times a month for several years. The pay was crap but the best thing it did was make me a better speaker, able to relate to a diverse group and think on my feet. Practice helps.

So practice. If you're The Boss, you owe it to your direct reports, your organization, and yourself. Invest in yourself and you'll benefit everyone around you.

"I have learned over the years that when one's mind is made up, this diminishes fear; knowing what must be done does away with fear."

Rosa Parks

Chapter 1
Quit Being Afraid!

"I was scheduled to make a year-end presentation to our board of directors covering the financial status of our bank. Although I was an administrative Vice President, I was the only woman board member to address the 12 men who sat on our board. I was a little nervous but had practiced at home and felt confident it would go well.

I stood up at the end of the long table facing the seated board members. I judiciously passed out the reports I was planning to review, but within only a few minutes of reviewing the financial reports, I experienced a hot flash that turned my face red and erupted a sweat I had never experienced before. I had to use Kleenex to stop the sweat dripping from my face. What to do??????? I stuttered and thought: these guys are going to think I am falsifying the records. So I thought I'd better go all the way...by faking a fainting spell! The president cancelled the meeting and one of the board members, a medical doctor, checked me out. He said it was stress. Although the meeting resumed the following week without incident, I never forgot it."

Mary Ale
Santa Ana, CA

Put yourself in Mary's shoes. Here is someone who was a senior executive, well versed in her job and seemingly well prepared for the presentation, but ended up experiencing a meltdown in front of her audience. However, she's not alone. Anne shares a similar experience:

"As the shift supervisor, it's my responsibility to brief the team at the beginning of a shift. I'll never forget my first one. Here I am, newly graduated from college addressing a group of mostly middle-aged men. Looking out into their frowning faces, I suddenly forgot what I was supposed to say. I drew a complete blank. Time slowed down to a crawl. It was like one of those dreams where you're being chased but you can't run because your buried up to your neck in Vaseline.

The only words that came out were 'do a good job today' and then I quickly left the group, went into the restroom and threw up. Fortunately, after talking to my dad later that morning, he talked me off the ledge of wanting to quit. He gave me a few tips and I did much better the next day. But nothing I learned in college speech classes prepared me for that first awful day!"

Anne White
Bluefield, WV

Are Mary and Anne unusual? Of course not! Time and time again, research has been done on the physical and mental effects fear of public speaking has on individuals. According to statistics, it's stronger than the fear of dying followed by financial ruin, and spiders & snakes. According to the Book of Lists, the fear of speaking in public is the #1 fear of all fears. The fear of dying is #7! Over 41% of people have some fear or anxiety dealing with speaking in front of groups.

More importantly, if you're The Boss, giving presentations is something you'll have to do all the time. People look to you for information and inspiration. If you can't communicate in front of a group, you're screwed. Then, what happens when you have to present your team's progress to the senior executives? If I work for you and you can't competently go up the chain to represent me and give me the resources I need to be successful, I'll lose all respect for you.

The Boss needs to be The Boss at presenting!

If it doesn't come natural, then you need to get busy working had to make it come natural. This book is full of helpful tips on how to do that. We'll start by addressing the common reasons people are afraid of presenting and then we'll build a winning structure to prepare and deliver a knockout presentation. The advice is here, but you'll have to be the one to put it into practice. I know you can do it!

But first, let's look at the most common reasons people fear giving a presentation. The same people that collect research on the fear of public speaking generally agree on the following reasons for the fear. We'll refer to them from here on as the **BIG EIGHT:**

1. Speaking in Public is Often Unfamiliar to Us

If you're afraid, is it because you don't get to speak often? Like most things in life, repetition tends to build confidence. If your opportunities to speak come seldom, perhaps once or twice in your high school speech class, then maybe with the toast you gave at your best friend's wedding, it's no wonder you may be dreading that upcoming presentation!

2. We Lack Confidence

Strangely enough, we are usually asked to present something because we know more about it than others do! If this is true, the audience should be clamoring for our every word! Why then are we worried about what the audience will think? In this case, I believe the answer is that we are unaccustomed to the pedestal the audience puts us on. It could be a low self- esteem issue, a pervasive negative atmosphere, or even a culture of "listening to refute" rather than just plain old listening. Whatever the case, we tend to discount the information power we have and focus on the microscope we believe the audience is viewing us with.

3. We Feel Isolated

Being in the spotlight may be something we all fantasize about, but the reality is that it's pretty scary! On stage, we know everyone is looking at us. The focus is solely on us. Our voice is amplified through a microphone. Our presence has been announced and anticipated for hours, days, or even months. There's no support for us up there, just us, our notes, maybe a PowerPoint® slide presentation to distract the audience from time to time, but nothing else. Isolation away from people is one thing, but isolation with everyone watching YOU can be terrifying.

4. We're Naturally Self-Conscious

Do you have an accent? Does your voice carry a low or high pitch? Do you move your arms when you speak or hold them tightly to your sides? Do you move your feet around or stand very still? If the answer is YES to any of those questions, then realize that you share these same traits with the other nine billion people on the Earth! We are all unique, yet all have some of the same characteristics when we get in front of an audience. But when we are amplified, spotlighted, and the focus of the attention, we often believe we are the most unique individuals ever seen.

5. We're Afraid of Looking Foolish

If you think back on all the presentations or speeches you've seen, you probably recall different incidents where the speaker looked nervous, had their fly open, tripped on a cord on their way up to the podium, or any other number of unfortunate, embarrassing experiences. In every case, you probably whispered to yourself I'm sure glad that isn't ME up there! The problem is, NOW YOU ARE UP THERE! Every one of those memories will now reappear as you prepare for your presentation.

6. We're Afraid of the Consequences

If our presentation is lousy, we'll forever be judged by it. If we've been able to fake our expertise in private, we'll now be exposed in public. Even if we do well, we may have to get up and repeat the performance somewhere else!

7. We're Afraid of Making Mistakes

Maybe you remember sitting in a presentation where the speaker made a major mistake, quoted an incorrect source, or completely forgot their lines. While similar to Fear #5, this fear is different in that in many ways it's subtle – you wonder who, if anyone caught it – and the pressure of NOT knowing drives you crazy!

8. We're Afraid We'll Be Boring

Boring speakers are not only ineffective, but also cement that trademark into their reputation. If our subject matter is intrinsically important to us, there's no greater insult than to have an audience bored by it. We fear having any presentation we give be prophesied in advance with statements such as "oh no, not that same boring speaker again."

Each of the **BIG EIGHT** is completely valid. I've experienced all of them and think about them every time I teach a class or give a presentation. The difference now is that rather than be paralyzed by them, I'm now propelled by them.

How is this possible? It happens when you separate fear from adrenaline.

What is fear? Webster defines it as: "A feeling of agitation and anxiety caused by the presence or imminence of danger."

What is the danger? When it comes to public speaking, there really is no inherent danger, just the anticipation of danger. Essentially, our fear of public speaking is more a fear of possible, POTENTIAL problems rather than actual problems. This holds true even if you've never had bad experiences in the past. The anticipation of every possible negative, horrible scenario haunts us, from the day we are asked to give the presentation, through the preparation phase, and of course in the moments leading up to our appearance on stage. And ALL of this is based on something that hasn't even happened yet! Does that mean it isn't real? Of course not, but it does give us hope that we can change our mental state to override the fear.

Adrenaline is different. Technically speaking, adrenaline is a hormone produced by the adrenal medulla in mammals. It causes quickening of the heartbeat, strengthens the force of the heart's contraction, opens the bronchioles in the lungs and has numerous other effects.

The secretion of adrenaline is part of the "fight-or-flight" reaction that we have in response to being frightened. With this better blood flow towards the skeletal muscles and liver, the muscles and liver will be able to function to their highest ability do to the increase in oxygen that they are receiving. This explains the stories you've probably heard where a frail grandmother lifts a car off her grandson, freeing him after the floor jack fails and causes the car to collapse. It's a positive charge that spurs us to athletic excellence. It may be the same feeling you get in your stomach when you see an e-mail or text message pop up on your screen from somebody special.

In a presentation, adrenaline is the boost of energy we need to override the fear of potential problems and deliver an energetic and motivating presentation. Of course, this energy must be harnessed – otherwise our presentation may frighten the audience. But if we leverage adrenaline to work in the right amount, and in the right place, the results can be awesome!

How do we tap into this? We'll work on it at length in this book but for now just realize that each of us has this power within us. If we combine it with meticulous preparation and a strong base of knowledge in our subject matter, we can't possibly fail!

"I have self-doubt. I have insecurity. I have fear of failure. I have nights when I show up at the arena and I'm like, 'My back hurts, my feet hurt, my knees hurt. I don't have it. I just want to chill.' We all have self-doubt. You don't deny it, but you also don't capitulate to it. You embrace it."

Kobe Bryant

Chapter 2
Acknowledge

The first step in our journey is to **acknowledge** what skills and abilities we already possess. It seems like a logical process. After all, professional sports teams assess talent each year before training camp to see which skilled players they have and where the needs might be. If a business process is going to be improved, baseline metrics must be established. If someone wants to implement a new fitness routine, they should start by assessing where they currently are.

Improving our ability to speak confidently in front of a crowd is no different. Our first job is to see what strengths and abilities we already have. If you've never taken the time to do this, you'll be shocked at how much of a "natural" you already are! You may also be surprised that in spite of your preferences, your abilities may be quite strong. Either way, a period of introspection is a wonderful way to start.

Let's look at some of the basic areas we need to acknowledge as we work to build our speaking skills:

1. Our Personality Preference or Type
2. Our Presentation Style
3. Our Fear

What's My Preference?

How well do you know yourself? Do you affirm comments, observations, criticisms, and feedback others give you?

These questions are important to answer if we want to acknowledge who we are and what have inside of us. In fact, we need to know this if we ever want to find out why we may have any of the **Big Eight** we talked about in Chapter One.

When you watch other presenters, do you notice that some have a knack for taking a very obscure concept and making it understandable? How about others who can generate lots of energy with their mere presence on stage? Do you notice some speakers who have the ability to deliver potentially bad news while making every effort to connect with the emotions of those in the audience?

If this seems natural for some presenters, it's possible their personality preference or Type is one reason why. I believe that each of us comes "pre-wired" at birth with certain personality preferences. But while we have "pre-wired" preferences that make it easier to present, skills, we also have the ability to either develop the skills that don't come naturally to us. It all comes down to a preference. We prefer one thing over another, but we can still do that non-preferred thing if we push ourselves really hard.

For breakfast, would you rather eat a donut or an apple?

If you prefer donuts, you'd probably eat an apple if you had to, but given the choice, you prefer a donut. Personality preferences are the same. You prefer one thing but if you had to, you could do the opposite.

Here are four ways to break down our personality preferences.

What Activities Energize Me?

Take a moment and think about the following questions:

- In a large group, are you the one making introductions, or do you like to be introduced?

- When you're with a group of people, would you prefer to talk with the group, or talk individually with people you know?

- Is it easy for you to talk to almost anyone for as long as you have to, or do you find a lot to say only to certain people or under certain conditions?

Your answers to these questions help determine whether you have a preference for Introversion or an Extraversion. People with a preference for Extraversion *(and notice that we use "a preference for" in how we describe these. I would not call you a donut if you had a preference for donuts at breakfast)* tend to prefer verbalization, big crowds, and multiple relationships. They're most often found seeking the company of others, and find it difficult to get anything done in total isolation and silence. It's because those things give them energy.

People with a preference for Introversion are quite different. They tend to seek depth and appears quiet and reflective. They're most often found working quietly and efficiently behind closed doors and large groups of people tend to wear them out. Since extraversion and introversion address energy flow, you'll most often find them cheerful and refreshed after spending hours toiling in their preferred environment.

A word of caution though. While this one appears to be easy to spot, you might be surprised to see the amount of energetic, outgoing motivational speakers who are actually prefer Introversion! They simply know how to channel their energy out of their comfortable preference and into the situation that demands it. And, at the end of a long day spent in front of crowds, they become physically exhausted. I speak from experience here!

How do I Gather my Information?

Now take a moment and think about the following questions:

- Would you rather hang around someone who is always coming up with new ideas, or thinks "inside the box?"

- When you read, do you enjoy odd or original ways of saying things, or do you wish writers would describe things as they are?

- Are you more intrigued by theory or do you prefer a more scientific approach?

- Are you one of those people who don't believe things until you can process them with your five senses or do you trust your gut?

Your answers to these questions tell us if you prefer to gather information through Sensing or iNtuition.

Generally speaking, people with a preference for Sensing prefer to gather information in the here and now, literally, perhaps using the five senses. If you ask them to describe an object such as an orange, they'll look at just THAT particular orange, smell it, peel it, taste it, and then describe THAT orange only. They're most comfortable with data they can completely account for.

Folks with a preference for INtuition on the other hand, tend to gather their information figuratively, looking perhaps for relationships, possibilities, and additional meanings. If you hand people with this preference an orange, they'll certainly hold it and look at it, but don't be surprised if they begin describing oranges. They'll talk about the climate to grow oranges in, which may include California or Florida, then they'll talk about the vacation they took to Disney World, which leads them to a discussion of the best time they ever had as a family, etc.

Which Part of Me Makes Decisions?

Think about these questions:

- Do you prefer sentimental things over more logical things, or vice versa?

- Does you find it difficult to empathize with someone's experience?

- Do you consider facts or people's feelings or opinions when making an important decision?

Your choices here help determine whether you use emotion or logic when it comes to making decisions. We can refer to you as having a preference for Thinking Or Feeling.

If you have a preference for Thinking, it doesn't mean you're smart. It just means you prefer to make decisions based on objective data. For you, fairness, clarity, and justice are key descriptors of your process. You tend to look at the consequences of the action and use them to help decide the necessary course of action.

If you prefer Feeling, you make your decisions differently. You're primarily motivated by relationships and interpersonal factors. The impact of the decision on the people involved is the driving force in your choices. While at first glance this preference may come across as tentative and not as confident as the preferred thinker might, it's important to realize that once both make a decision, it's firm and unbending. The process sets the two apart.

How Do I Prefer to Structure My Life?

Now try to answer these questions:

- Do you plan events well in advance, or prefer to do whatever looks like fun when the time comes?

- When you have an important task at hand, do you like to organize it carefully before you start, or plan it as you go along?

- Would you prefer to do most things according to what feels right, or a set schedule?

Depending on how you answered those four questions, we might tell if you prefer lots of structure and closure (Judging), or prefer less of a rigid environment (Perceiving).

People with a preference for Judging like neatness, conciseness, and a clearly defined finish line. They are list-makers and are likely to use a day planner and stick with it year-round. In terms of preference, they would most likely prefer to be decision-makers rather than information-gatherers.

People who have a preference for Perceiving like less formal systems, instead opting to address situations as they arise. Give someone like this a leather organizer and it will gather dust. Let them have a calendar app and they'll ignore it, opting to check social media instead. For them, closure only comes when all the data and plans are ready – this defines the deadline. They don't appreciate YOU setting the deadline for them. They can work well under pressure if it's their pressure. These folks certainly have structure, but it's their structure and it fits them and their Type.

How Do You Get All That Information From A Few Questions – And Is It Valid?

Much of the work done around Type was pioneered by Swiss-born Psychiatrist C.G. Jung, who hypothesized that human behavior didn't just "happen", but was related to a set of preferences that are established early in life and form the basis of the personality that others see. As a person gets older, much of what they do, see, and think is framed by those preferences. Jung's work was then built upon by Katherine Briggs and her daughter, Isabel Briggs-Myers. They developed an assessment containing similar questions to the ones you previously answered, and the results give your preferences based on the following table:

Discovering your Type is accomplished by taking this particular assessment, which is known as the Myers-Briggs Type Indicator (MBTI)®.

The MBTI® is statistically sound and designed to measure your self-identified preferences. The instrument has been around for decades and currently taken by over two million people each year. You really can get all that information from those 93 questions!

So What?

Understanding your personality Type and preferences is the first step to acknowledging why you might fear public speaking. We often fear what we don't understand. If you have difficulty interacting with large groups of people, or if doing so really tires you out, it's helpful to know that it might be because you have a preference for Introversion. You can give an outstanding presentation with ease when you run through it in your head, or when you give it to a small familiar group of two or three people, but transitioning that onto the stage is troublesome.

Similarly, if you have trouble taking large and confusing concepts and making them understandable to a diverse audience, or if you have a tendency to drone on and on with the same point and say the same thing a thousand different ways, this could be a result of preference for either Sensing or iNtuition.

If, when delivering a presentation that could negatively impact the current conditions of the people around you, and you come across as cold and calloused, or emotional and overly-concerned; we might say it's because you're playing into your Thinking or Feeling preference.

You might be one of those presenters who can stick to your allotted time or run way ahead of it. On the other hand, you might have a tendency to run over the time, perhaps getting caught up in a question and answer time that leads to more discussion. If either of these apply, it's probably due to you're either practicing Judging or Perceiving.

Each of these four dichotomies is extremely helpful when doing the basic assessment of your SELF. While we're essentially stuck with our preferences for life, we don't have to be held prisoner by them. Whether speaking in front of a group seems natural or not, we can all learn to shift out of our preferences in order to get to a strong comfort level. We'll talk about that more in later in the book.

Points to Ponder

1. Do I have a preference for Introversion or Extraversion?

2. Do I have a preference for Sensing or iNtuition?

3. Do I have a preference for Thinking or Feeling?

4. Do I have a preference Judging or Perceiving?

What's My Style?

If you decided to become a professional boxer, your first step, the one before drinking raw eggs and getting up before dawn to run, would be to assess your boxing style. Your coach and manager would analyze your punch strength, speed, boxing ability, and conditioning. Only after observing this through hours of training and sparring, would your management team agree you were ready for your first fight.

What's your presentation style? Do you prefer to interact with your audience, or would you rather deliver information in a lecture? Are you mobile up on stage, or do you prefer a stationary place, safely behind a podium? Are you comfortable with using metaphors, or would you rather just give the information straight and to the point? Do you like high-tech visual aids, or would a simple flip chart and note cards suit you?

The Elements of Style

Each of these questions is designed to help you learn more about your presentation style. We all have preferences for how we would ideally like to present. If we master our style, we'll become quite comfortable presenting information in an environment that suits us. What are the elements of style? We have some suggestions below. See which of these seem comfortable to you.

Use of Pace & Pauses

How fast do you speak? Do you have a tendency to run your sentences together very quickly, or are you more deliberate?

Pace is the speed at which we speak. It's a little like running a mile. If you begin very quickly, only to finish slowly, we might say that you failed to "pace yourself." Speaking is the same way. If you tend to begin quickly, then blow through your hours' worth of material in five minutes, your pace may be too fast. If you have only 20 minutes to speak, but end up consistently running over your allotted time, we might say your pace is too slow.

Pauses are the natural spots for us to take a breath of air when we speak. In writing, a comma signals a logical place to take a breath – which helps us better structure our written work. If your presentation seems to run smoothly, yet you constantly find yourself "out of synch" when trying to catch your breath, it may be a result of ill-timed or poorly planned pauses. We'll see a little later how a well-timed, strategically placed pause can have more impact than the word that it precedes.

Voice Modulation

When you listen to game show host, actor, and commentator Ben Stein, do you think he comes across as boring? If so, it's probably because he speaks in a very deliberate, monotone voice. He's a brilliant man, but to the average person, the brilliance is heavily cloaked in a presentation voice that prevents us from hearing what he has to say.

Voice modulation is the act of changing our tone and pitch to keep our audience listening. It involves emphasizing certain syllables, words, and phrases. If you want a good example of good voice modulation, watch a TV preacher sometime. Their emotional appeal is most often contained in a well-timed voice inflection. Martin Luther King Jr.'s *I Have A Dream* speech is a wonderful example of voice modulation in action. While Dr. King's words are indeed powerful on their own, I doubt Ben Stein could make the same impact in his monotone delivery.

Eye Contact

Making eye contact is a critical part of getting your message across. In some cultures, eye contact is in itself a greeting, an acknowledgement of your pure existence. In particular, the tribes of northern Natal in South Africa greet each other with Sawu bona, a salutation that literally means "I see you." If we have a bad customer service experience, many times it begins because a clerk fails to maintain eye contact with us.

I remember a speaker we had back in high school on chapel day. During his 30-minute sermon, he looked over our heads and failed to make eye contact even once. I had no clue what he was trying to say, mainly because I felt he wasn't trying to talk to me anyway. Good eye contact tells your audience that YOU have an important message specifically tailored to their ears. The pathway to the audience's soul is through the ears, but you must first get through the gateway of the eyes.

Learning to make eye contact is a challenge for most of us. Maybe it's because we grew up listening to our parents tell us "it's not polite to stare." Perhaps we think it's confrontational. People tell me to never make eye contact with a growling dog as they see it as a challenge.

One way to ease into using eye contact is to practice the two-second rule. As you speak, make eye contact with each person in the audience for two seconds at a time. If you're up on stage, you won't actually have to look them in the eyes, just look at their forehead. Make a conscious effort to speak and scan the crowd, with two-second stops at as many people you can. Be sure to scan gently; don't dart all over the room. Take care not to focus on one person or section for too long. I always find it difficult to move from someone who appears to be very interested in what I'm saying. Also, be careful not to get sidetracked by individuals in the audience that may get our attention. It could be a person we know who makes a surprise appearance, or maybe someone in bright colored clothes, or maybe a person with a physical abnormality. In these cases, it most certainly is impolite to stare, plus we'll probably lose our train of thought.

Later, we'll talk about strategies to help us learn about our audience before even stepping out on stage, which should prevent any audience anomalies from surprising us.

Gestures

Have you ever met people who convince you they'd be mute if you tied their hands behind their back? Each of us speaks with some gestures, some of us more than others.

The use of natural gestures in a presentation gives it variety, works to emphasize certain points, and helps us connect with those who are watching us. It's the non-verbal equivalent of voice modulation. Do you remember President Clinton's vehement denial of his relationship with Monica Lewinsky in the late 1990s? What stood out to most observers was his pointed finger gesturing as he emphasized,

"I did not...have sexual relations...with that woman... Miss Lewinsky."

When it comes to using gestures, moderation is key. Too much can wear an audience out, too little lulls them to sleep. Again, take a look at TV preachers to get an idea which amount is right for you.

Here is a final word about gestures. Be sure to choose them carefully. In high school, Mr. May, our school administrator was giving a rather animated lecture in a Bible class when he raised up his hand to point upward and used his middle finger rather than his index finger. Of course the class mentally checked out after that – we couldn't believe Mr. May gave us all The Finger.

Posture & Body Language

Several years ago, a study was published in which former street muggers observed videotapes featuring normal citizens walking down the street. They were asked which of these they would choose to assault if they were still involved in their evil past. The observers overwhelmingly chose to avoid people that had body language and posture that exuded confidence. This could be anything from walking erect with shoulders back, hands swinging naturally at their sides, and head not locked forward, but naturally aware of the surroundings.

Body language is the most powerful communication we have. It can be argued that every body movement has a meaning and no movement is accidental. For example, through body language we say "Help me, I'm lonely"; "Take me, I'm available"; or "Leave me alone, I'm depressed." We rarely send our non-verbal messages consciously. We lift one eyebrow for disbelief. We rub our noses for puzzlement. We fold our arms to protect ourselves. We shrug our shoulders for indifference, wink one eye for intimacy, tap our fingers for impatience, and slap our forehead for forgetfulness.

Posture is important too. Good posture accomplishes two objectives. First, good posture, i.e. shoulders back, head high, arms naturally at the side exudes confidence. You're the expert – your body language says that for you. It's more powerful than a bio tucked inside the course materials. Secondly, good posture helps you breath, which in turn allows you to have better modulation, breath more naturally, and make your strategic pauses where you need them.

Just as with gestures, body language can either energize our presentation, put the audience to sleep, or create total confusion as you gyrate all over the stage. Don't overdo it. You're not in the audience at a wrestling match or a Tony Robbins event. Be reasonable and appropriate.

Appropriate body language consists what we've covered previously about eye contact and gestures, but with the added act of a conscious smile. After eye contact, the presence or absence of a smile sends a very important message:

"I'm glad to be here and I like you."

There's no better way to get your audience connected to you than with a smile. Of course the key is to have a sincere smile. Your audience won't be fooled. Let them know you are excited to be there and that you like them!

Filler Words & Nervous Habits

What is "um?" It's a filler word – a word we use to fill in a "dead spot" in the presentation. "Um" isn't the only culprit. "Ya know" is another biggie. Watch professional athletes in an interview and you'll see this one used liberally. "Uh" makes a nice filler too. Teenagers like "like." Entrepreneurs like to start every sentence and answer any question with "so." In any place where silence seems uncomfortable, the filler word finds a home.

Filler words are sometimes impossible to eliminate, but we can certainly make an effort to minimize them. One way is to appreciate the pause. Use that quiet moment to make emphasis, gather your thoughts, or prepare the audience for the next phrase. There's nothing wrong with a little silence, provided it's no longer than a second or so. Another way is to have a trusted person count your filler words. You'll be surprised how often and how naturally filler words invade your presentation.

Each of us has nervous habits. I'm not sure where they come from, but we all have nervous tics that happen when we experience stress.

The late comedian Rodney Dangerfield tugged at the knot in his tie. Jack Nicholson smoothed his eyebrows. Professional baseball players possess and perform a wide array of nervous habits, from "crossing" themselves, to spitting, to tugging on the bill of their caps. Why is this?

Nervous habits are like filler words. We use them to fill in a break in the action where a spoken word is either inappropriate or impossible to use. It usually happens when we are the focus of attention. While some folks enjoy the spotlight, others feel much too vulnerable in it, and manifest this feeling by doing some sort of gesture. It's almost always unconscious. I never knew I twisted my rings when I was teaching until a student mentioned it to me. Sometimes we use nervous habits as a ritual – much like a good luck charm. Just remember that both filler words and nervous habits are usually evident to everyone but YOU. Enlist the help of some trusted friends to help point them out to you.

Enjoyment and Ease

Do you like your audience and the subject you're presenting? If so, it probably shows through your non-verbal language more than anything else. Aside from eye contact, a smile, and positive voice modulation, nothing communicates your enjoyment and ease more than your apparent comfort level with the audience.

This is difficult – after all, you may be experiencing sheer terror on the inside, but the outside must not show it. Take a look at some of the better talk show hosts on television. I'm sure each of them experiences nerves while on camera, but you'd never know it from watching them. Jerry Springer calmly moves about the stage in spite of angry women clawing at each other's clothes and hair. Dr. Phil McGraw maintains composure even when you know he wants to reach out and slap some of his guests. Oprah Winfrey expresses extreme compassion and anger without coming off as overly emotional. Why? Each of them is at ease with their audience. They are the experts - they are in control. How do you master this skill? It comes from knowledge, preparation, and practice. We'll cover this more in later in the book.

So What's YOUR Style?

Now that you know what's involved in presentation style, the next step is to find YOUR style. The best way is to ask others for feedback. Take a look at evaluations from previous presentations you've made. Find out from trusted friends and colleagues where your strengths were – this will indicate where you were able to operate well within your comfort level – most likely when you were working in your preferred style.

But what if you've never presented before? If this is your first time, perhaps a couple of dry runs in front of a small and friendly audience would be helpful. Ask for honest feedback. Find out what got and held their attention. If you can't get that audience together or are not yet ready for prime time, then try watching a video of you presenting.

A video won't lie to you. It's a great way to see yourself from the audience's perspective. The only requirement is that you can do an honest self-assessment of your style based on what you observe.

Just as a fighter must learn their own style, maximizing it to their benefit, they must also learn to adjust whenever necessary. The fighter's manager can sometimes pick opponents that are suited to their style, but often they have very little choice. You may have little choice of presenting under the conditions most appealing to you – so mastering multiple styles is an important skill to learn.

Points to Ponder

1. What is my style?

2. What areas do I need to develop?

3. Who can I trust to help find my strengths and weaknesses?

Facing Your Fear

All of us have some fear of presenting. The key question is to ask why? If we know specifically what we fear, we can take steps to conquer it.

If you fear giving a presentation, ask yourself this series of questions:

- What was the worst experience I ever had giving a presentation?
- What was the reason that particular experience happened?
- Did I learn from that experience?
- What is the ONE thing I fear most that might happen during upcoming or future presentations?
- If that ONE thing happens, what will the fallout be?
  Will that fallout result in death or personal injury to me or anyone I love?
- Am I willing to face my fears and develop strategies to overcome them?

Remember our thoughts about fear in Chapter One? Fear is really nothing more than the anxiety that comes from possible, POTENTIAL problems rather than actual problems. While this should provide you a measure of comfort, let me elaborate for those who are still nervously biting their nails.

It seems like the natural reaction to express fear when we're called on to do a presentation. After all, we don't want to come across as cocky. It's also a natural reaction to begin sweating and getting nervous and afraid when our dentist comes into the exam room and the assistant unwraps the sharp instruments. We haven't yet experienced pain today, but perhaps we had a bad experience before which scares us. It seems as though our brain works overtime to scare us! Why does this happen?

To understand how this works, we have to take a look at classical conditioning, one of the many ways that humans learn.

Classical conditioning grew out of experiments conducted at the turn of the twentieth century by Russian physiologist, Ivan Pavlov. Working closely with his dog, Pavlov determined that learning a conditioned response involves building up an association between a conditioned stimulus, and an unconditioned stimulus. How does this work? In Pavlov's experiment, he would blow some powdered meat into his dog's face, which caused the dog to salivate. This is what we might call the unconditioned stimulus. Dogs will salivate at the scent and taste of food. Then Pavlov began ringing a bell at the same time he blew the meat into the dog's face. Eventually, all it took was the ringing bell to get the dog drooling. This response was a result of the conditioned stimulus – that of the ringing bell.

What does that mean for us? It's very simple. Just as some of us had bad experiences in the dentist's office previously and now begin to get nervous when we smell the topical anesthetic and see the instruments, we also begin to visualize actual or imagined bad experiences during a presentation. We replay the scenario over and over, until like Pavlov's dog, we begin to respond as if the unconditioned stimulus was upon us. Maybe we envision ourselves up on the stage and the audience is laughing at us. We may see ourselves dropping our notes, or the nervously stalling for time when the PowerPoint® slides freeze up. Perhaps we see ourselves losing our train of thought and drawing a complete blank. Worst of all, we imagine a hostile audience, listening only to respond, and then beating us up during the question and answer period.

QUIT SALIVATING AT THE SOUND OF THE RINGING BELL!!!

You're much brighter than Pavlov's dog and can choose to break this cycle! We'll work on it together! You can no doubt fill up several sheets of paper with potential problems. I can too. The difference is that we'll address them and overcome them through careful preparation and flawless execution. We'll plan our work and work our plan. It will happen through a combination of self-awareness, mental conditioning, audience scouting, and practice. Let's transform that fear into useful adrenaline and deliver a knockout presentation!

Points to Ponder

1. What was the worst experience I ever had giving a presentation?

2. What was the reason that particular experience happened?

3. Did I learn from that experience?

4. What is the ONE thing I fear most that might happen during upcoming or future presentations?

5. If that ONE thing happens, what will the fallout be?

6. Will that fallout result in death or personal injury to me or anyone I love?

7. Am I willing to face my fears and develop strategies to overcome them?

"Failure isn't an option. I've erased the word 'fear' from my vocabulary, and I think when you erase fear, you can't fail."

Alicia Keys

Chapter 3
Planning

Zig Ziglar, in his book *See You At The Top*, recounts the story of and Air Force pilot, Major Nesmith. Nesmith was an average golfer who routinely shot in the high nineties at his favorite course. In the late 1960's he took a seven-year break from the game. During this time, he became separated from his family and friends, and his health deteriorated. Amazingly, when he resumed playing after his hiatus, he managed to shoot a 74 on his course on the first time back out! How did this happen?

Nesmith was one of many Americans held as a prisoner of war in North Vietnam. During his time in captivity, much of which was spent in solitary confinement, he passed the hours away by returning mentally to that same golf course. He visualized each detail, even down to getting dressed in his golfing clothes. He imagined himself at every tee, played in different weather conditions, and "saw" each ball he hit in real time. Nesmith didn't miss a detail, even going so far as to coach himself on proper hand placement and swing mechanics. He counted off the steps from the tee box to where his ball was on the fairway.

In seven years, he played a four-hour game every day. During this time, he never missed a shot. Each drive was powerful, straight, and landed exactly where he wanted it. His putting was flawless.

Is it any wonder that he could then come back after that absence and shoot a 74? Of course not! Zig Ziglar points out, "If you want to reach your goal, you must actually "see the reaching" in your own mind before you actually arrive at the goal."

Does the same principle work for giving presentations? Of course! The concept of visualizing is nothing new. Athletes have been using it for years. If you've ever found yourself daydreaming, or having an "out of body" experience, you've been doing it as well.

For our purposes, visualizing is the first step in the Planning process. Most of us visualize backwards! We imagine ourselves in front of the group and picture everything going wrong. Is our poor performance then a self-fulfilling prophecy? It could be. Take a look at the following scenario:

"I'm sitting in the front row, nervously awaiting my turn at the podium. The nervousness though is focused – I'm prepared and I'm ready! I was asked to present in front of this group because I'm an expert in my field. Nobody else knows the subject, they always come to me with questions. My notes are carefully prepared, but I won't even need them, for I have rehearsed this presentation a hundred times over. There's no need to worry

about the PowerPoint slides, I don't have any. My audience wants to hear from me, not a fancy animated word display.

I'm now being introduced. The audience applauds. I make my way to the podium, confidently lay my notes down, and deliver my well-rehearsed opening line. My voice is strong and confident. There is no quivering, no throat clearing, no "ums." The audience is in my hand. They are putty before me. I'm shaping them with my every word. Each of my points are clear, my illustrations vivid. I make eye contact with all of them. Forget that nonsense about seeing them in their underwear, I see their eyes.

The time passes so quickly up here. I begin to wind down and deliver a powerful conclusion. The audience stands and applauds. The questions and answer period now begins. What a wonderful experience. My audience (yes, they are mine – I molded them with my words) has obviously listened to learn. They ask me questions that appear to be unanswerable to them, but the answers roll off my tongue. Heads nod in approval, and copious notes are being taken. I am the expert and they appreciate my sharing a few moments with them.

Alas, the time is up. Once again I hear thunderous applause. I quickly and gracefully move off the stage and out the back door. It was an incredible experience!"

Does this sound like something you want to experience? If so, let me assure you that it WILL happen! If you visualize your upcoming event using the same technique, you cannot help but have an awesome experience.

However the visualizing does not itself deliver the knockout. Preparation is imperative. This chapter will take you step by step through the planning and preparation process. Continue to visualize, but let's start with the basics.

What's My Goal For This Presentation – And Which Type of Presentation Should I Make?

The first step in preparation is to figure out the end result or the goal. This is probably easy, after all, either you volunteered to speak for a particular reason, or somebody asked you to speak. If the latter was the case, I'm sure you asked, "What exactly are you looking for from my presentation?" Remember, either you asked to speak because you are an expert in the topic, or somebody asked you because they thought you were the expert. In either case, you are in charge – this presentation will be YOUR show, so plan it accordingly.

While most experts give a host of presentation types, I believe they all come down to three main formats. Keeping your goal in mind, choose from the following:

1. Informative
2. Persuasive
3. Teaching/Training

Informative Presentations

Informative presentations serve to share information. Some examples might be:

- Telling employees about a change in benefits
- Informing shareholders of annual profit figures
- Explaining how a construction project will affect traffic and parking

Your goal in an informative presentation is to inform. In its purest form, the informative presentation presents data objectively and without emotion. Informative presentations are probably the most common. We see them everywhere from the White House press briefing room, to our own organizations when the CEO holds a town hall meeting.

There's no reason to persuade the audience, after all, what you are presenting is usually not up for debate. Of course this doesn't mean you can forget about planning and strategy. Secretly, you're still going to have to employ persuasive strategies. We'll cover this in a moment.

Persuasive Presentations

Persuasive presentations serve to convince your audience of something and get them moving forward on it. Some examples are:

- Convincing employees that the change in benefits is truly serving their best interest
- Demonstrating to shareholders how your past performance is a good indicator of future success
- Mobilizing employees to voluntarily and cheerfully park offsite or take public transportation during a construction project

Your goal in a persuasive presentation is to mobilize and move the audience forward. It's designed to convince them that your points are valid and they should rush to comply. We most often associate persuasive presentations with famous orators like Martin Luther King, Jr. and John F. Kennedy. Consider the following excerpt from this famous persuasive presentation:

"I have a dream that one day the state of Alabama, whose governor's lips are presently dripping with the words of interposition and nullification, will be transformed into a situation where little black boys and black girls will be able to join hands with little white boys and white girls and walk together as sisters and brothers. I have a dream today. I have a dream

that one day every valley shall be exalted, every hill and mountain shall be made low, the rough places will be made plain, and the crooked places will be made straight, and the glory of the Lord shall be revealed, and all flesh shall see it together. This is our hope. This is the faith with which I return to the South. With this faith we will be able to hew out of the mountain of despair a stone of hope. With this faith we will be able to transform the jangling discords of our nation into a beautiful symphony of brotherhood. With this faith we will be able to work together, to pray together, to struggle together, to go to jail together, to stand up for freedom together, knowing that we will be free one day."

Martin Luther King, Jr. August 28, 1963

Dr. King's speech mobilized a nation in pursuit of civil rights. It's a masterpiece of persuasion. More than 30 years later, it still gives us goose bumps as we view the black and white footage from that summer afternoon. You can almost hear his voice as you walk up the steps to the Lincoln Memorial in Washington, D.C.

Is it possible for you to give a persuasive presentation and have the same impact? Absolutely! We'll cover how to do it shortly.

Teaching/Training

Teaching and training is the last big category in presentation types. Your goal when teaching and training is to inform specifically, with action to follow. Aside from informative presentations, it's probably the most common. While they sound the same, teaching and training are quite different from each other. Consider the following examples of teaching:

- Leading your church's small group in a study of the book of Revelation.
- Lecturing on the principles of organizational behavior to a college class.
- Serving as a tour guide for your senior citizens group's museum tour.

Teaching covers large-scale overview concepts. It's like looking at a subject from 35 thousand feet. It's a more detailed version of the informative presentation.

Training is different. Take a look at the following examples:

- Showing your 16-year-old daughter how to drive a car with a manual transmission.
- Teaching your boss how to add an app to his smart phone.

- Demonstrating the finer points of housecleaning to your husband.

Training serves to impart a particular skill set to the audience. It's more common in small groups or maybe one-to-one, but you may find yourself giving an actual training session to a large group.

So Establish Your Goal!

The type of presentation you're making should help you decide the goal. In the education world, we often use learning objectives as the goal:

"By the end of this presentation, the audience will know how to..."

If you don't have objectives to use, then query the person who asked you to give the presentation. If they don't have anything specific in mind, you may have to set your own goals. It may be a good idea to work on some visualization. Imagine yourself in front of the audience again. Try to picture which part of the presentation gets them excited. If your goal is to inform, think about some ways to do MORE than inform – inspire them as well. If you have to persuade them, focus on the most positive points of the topic and build on them. If you have to teach or train, try to think of the most difficult parts of the subject and imagine some creative ways to talk about them. A good goal is the starting point, not the end point, on the road to presentation success!

Points to Ponder

1. What type of presentation will I be giving: Informative, Persuasive, or Teaching/Training?

2. Do I have a specific goal for this presentation?

3. If I have free reign over this presentation, which goal should I choose?

4. If I have been handed a set of expectations and a goal, how can I best work within them while still adding my own personality and creativity?

5. How well do you know your audience?

6. What Do I Know About My Audience?

"Shortly after starting my new business, a colleague that ran a monthly round table for a group of HR executives called and asked me to fill in for a speaker that had cancelled at the last minute. Grateful for the chance to present myself to a whole new group of peers, and hopefully prospects, I gladly accepted the invitation and asked my colleague for suggestions on presentation material and was told that anything I had ready would be welcome.

I had just finished a presentation for another group on how poor leadership, and specifically leader's failure to convey a clear organization vision contributed to the failure of teams in many organizations. My colleague said that this sounded fine to him and thanked me for filling in.

When I arrived at the presentation I found that my audience was far senior to me and not at all interested in my presentation. Fortunately, I realized that the only way to prevent a disaster was to allow the participants to add value to my presentation, just for their sheer pleasure. I became a facilitator asking for input on other's experiences surrounding my topic. We all won; they willingly contributed their collective wisdom, I learned from them, and all had a reasonably enjoyable time.

There are two lessons that I learned and that I wish to pass on for consideration. First and foremost, good presentations provide valuable information for the listeners. By simply delivering material that you have available like I did, I was trying to convince them to be interested in the topic that I was prepared to present, not on a topic that they were interested in. Good presentations not only give valuable information, but must fill a need of the audience.

This leads to my second lesson, refrain from speaking to a group without knowing the makeup of the group, their backgrounds and their interests. If you find yourself in this position, quickly become a FACILITATOR not a presenter. This allows them to determine the information that they need and seek it from the collective body of knowledge that includes not only the presenter, but also the other participants."

Karla Williams
Northbrook, IL

Karla's experience hammers home the following point:

KNOW YOUR AUDIENCE!

Remember our analogy of a fighter in training? After learning our own style, we then have to figure out the style of our opponent. Sometimes we learn it through a trainer, other times we might view highlights of their previous fights. There are of course some occasions where we might not know anything about our opponent, but will have to adapt in the ring.

For presentation purposes, knowing our audience is incredibly helpful, but not always possible. If we have access to someone who knows the audience, we can get the information from them. Sometimes (although I strongly encourage you NOT to) we just have to "wing it."

Knowing the audience sounds difficult, but really involves finding out just four things about the audience: learning style, values, attitudes, and beliefs. We'll break each one down individually.

Learning Styles

Learning theories abound and anyone in the education field no doubt has their favorite. I chose one of the easier-to-understand theories in order to help you grasp just some main points as you try to figure out the best way to reach an audience.

In 1982, Peter Honey and Alan Mumford classified adult learners in one of four ways:

Can you identify your particular learning preference from those four styles? Your learning style will certainly influence your presentation style, much like your personality preferences will. Additionally, it's important to realize you audience may all be listening to you, while learning from you in their own particular way. With that in mind, let's take a look at each one and develop some strategies to best appeal to them.

The Activist

Activists prefer a learning environment of "hands on." These are usually the folks that dig their new electronic gadget out of the box and immediately begin trying to hook it up. For them, the instruction manual is just a formality. They prefer to learn about their product by playing with it. Instruction manuals usually come later, and only if the activist gets totally stuck.

You may have some activists in your audience, so it's important to include, if at all possible, a few activities that will engage them during your presentation:

- Dialog and brainstorming
- Group discussions
- Competition
- Role playing

While you may not have the flexibility to actually engage the activists in your audience, it may be helpful to at least make your presentation somewhat interactive so as not to lose them.

The Reflector

Reflectors are a nervous presenter's best audience! They prefer to sit back and listen, then have some interactive activities to observe. If you decide to have an interactive presentation, use your activists to run the simulation, and have the reflectors be your observers. Most of the time, they will sit quietly and listen to you.

Reflectors are part of any audience, so you might want to be prepared for them by including some of the following activities if possible:

- Panel discussions
- Self-analysis and personality questionnaires
- Coaching and interviewing
- Observing activities

Even without having an interactive presentation, you can't help but appeal to a reflector. We'll cover some strategies later that will help you tailor to their needs.

The Theorist

Theorists are the audience members that make the unprepared speaker crash and burn. A theorist wants to know the details and in many cases might be listening to refute. However if you are completely prepared, and have mastered your subject, the theorists are a very rewarding group to speak to!

To connect to the theorists in your audience, you should include lots of the following in your presentation:

- Statistics
- Stories
- Quotations
- Background information
- Models

Remember, you were selected to present most likely because you're an expert in your subject. The theorists are waiting to hear from experts and if you prepare, you won't disappoint them.

The Pragmatist

Pragmatists are the thinking version of the activists. They too are very hands-on, but for them, they must get all of the information first and feel comfortable with it before diving in.

Activities that appeal to pragmatists are:

- Case studies
- Problem solving activities
- Discovery

- Time to think about how to apply the learning in reality

If you want to make your pragmatists happy, you must show them the relevance of your topic and give them an opportunity to answer the question, "what's in it for me?"

So What Should My Strategy Be?

Values and attitudes as we'll see shortly have a big role in the audience, but let me give you some tips on handling the four learning styles. This alone can help you better reach and hold your audience.

Let's assume an audience of 100 is equally divided into the four learning styles. You can easily take care of the activists by having copies of your materials and slides available before you begin. Remember, the activists tend to dive right in so as you begin the presentation, they are probably leafing through the materials and slides, far ahead of where you might be talking.

Your reflectors will be sitting back listening. Remember, they take in information and process it slowly. While some of them may appear uninterested, they're probably listening intently in their own fashion.

Your theorists and pragmatists should be the focus of your presentation. Remember, theorists prefer to hear the facts, figures, details, and maybe the supporting data. Pragmatists want to know "what's in it for them." These two groups are diametrically opposed, which means you have to speak to both. It sounds impossible, but really, it's quite simple. Toggle between each main point with a theorist/pragmatist focus. For example:

Theorist View:

"According to Carl Jung, human beings are predisposed to certain attitudes and functions. We are either born introverted or extraverted, or thinking and feeling. This should be paramount when designing incentive programs for employees."

Pragmatist View:

"So what am I saying here? If we are born a certain way, the chances of us changing when we enter an organization are slim. Be sure you get to know your people and what motivates them before you start handing out rewards."

I'm not repeating myself, just paraphrasing my statement to get the attention of the pragmatists. Remember, pragmatists are looking for the bottom line. They want enough information to get them out the door in order to test it and make sure it works.

While it may seem cumbersome, with practice it becomes quite natural. You don't need to paraphrase every statement, just the key points. These two groups will be the most vocal, both verbally and non-verbally so be sure to tune into them when speaking. If you do this right, the only folks who will ask questions at the end will be the reflectors. Be prepared to answer questions from all areas of your presentation (we'll cover that a little later in the book), and be patient with the activists who ask questions that you've already answered three times. Remember, they have probably spent the majority of the time reading ahead.

Final Thoughts on Learning Styles

We rarely have a choice in selecting our audiences. You may actually know many of the people who will be listening to you, but perhaps have never thought about their personality preferences or their learning style. If you've ever experienced a time where a presentation put you to sleep, it may have been because it didn't strike your learning style. Now that you know, be sure to at least try to cater to each of the four styles in some way. We'll talk about that a little later in the book.

Values and Attitudes

There are two other important areas to consider when planning to connect with your audience. Aside from personality and learning style, each member of your audience carries deeply rooted values and somewhat transparent attitudes. While they are somewhat similar concepts, each one has a uniqueness that at least bears some consideration. Failure to consider them could spell disaster – which you'll experience during your question and answer period!

Values

Values are the tenants each of us operate by. Values are essentially the very last thing you would ever give up. What we hold on to dearest is a good indicator of where our "heart" lies. Here's another way to look at it. Whenever we "draw a line in the sand," everything on our side of the line probably is, or directly relates to our values. We forbid anyone to cross over and tamper with them.

Values lay the foundation for the understanding of attitudes and motivation because they influence our perceptions. What we see as right and wrong is merely external data measured against our value systems.

When we speak to an audience, not only do we need to concern ourselves with their personality and learning styles, we also need to think about their values. If our topic is even remotely touches on religion or politics, we open ourselves up to the possibility of crossing someone's "line in the sand." Both of these topics are heavily rooted in individual values.

Attitudes

If values are the core motivators in individuals, then attitudes are the end results visible to the rest of us. We've often heard someone referred to as "having an attitude", but what does that really mean? To understand attitudes, we have to carefully consider the value system, for attitudes are the statements or behaviors that flow from them.

We've already talked about the deeply rooted values each of us carries. Regardless of where they came from, they influence much of our lives. Attitudes then, reflect how we feel about something. I like to refer to attitudes as "values with legs." They are the action component and are expressed cognitively (through opinions), affectively (through emotions), or behaviorally (through actions).

While values usually remain unchanged as we age, attitudes are more fluid. In fact, many different stimuli and environments influence them. Most radio and television ads work hard to change your attitude, knowing full well that your values probably won't budge.

What does this mean for you as a presenter? You can certainly try to appeal to your audience to change their attitude, but you'll need to keep their value systems in mind. Persuasive presentations need to make full use of appealing to change attitudes without attempting to alter values.

Why Bother With All This Touchy-Feely Stuff?

Planning to connect with the audience is key. You may be able to "wing it" with other parts of the presentation and get away with it, but don't attempt to do it here. Any bad experiences you may have had before could have come from not knowing your audience and appealing to just one small part of them. If you have any opportunity to find out about the audience in advance, please take advantage of it. It's the only way to guarantee success, and it's crucial when planning your presentation outline.

Points to Ponder

1. When thinking about prior presentations, can I identify people I know by their learning style?

2. Which learning style do I have?

3. Which learning style can I connect with the easiest?

4. What strategies can I work on in order to reach the other three learning styles?

5. What are my values and attitudes?

Getting Down to Business – Planning the Presentation Outline

So far we've spent a lot of time thinking about the type of presentation we'll do, our goal for the presentation, and the audience who will listen to the presentation. Now it's time to start assembling our materials. The best way to begin is with an outline.

All of us probably remember outlining speeches in middle school and high school. We often transferred that information onto 3x5 note cards. The purpose of that exercise was to help us organize our thoughts and materials.

This method works just as well today! Think of your outline as the skeleton on which you'll build your entire presentation.

What Makes Up The Outline?

An outline consists of four main sections:

1. The Objective
2. The Introduction
3. The Body
4. The Conclusion

The body itself may have several points underneath, but for right now let's figure out what goes specifically under the four main sections. How do you figure out what goes where? There is an easy formula to use:

1. Know what you're planning to tell them

2. Tell them what you're going to tell them.

3. Tell them

4. Tell them what you just told them

Sound simple enough? It really IS that simple! Of course we have to "flesh out" that skeleton a bit, but if we keep these four ideas in mind, we can't go wrong.

The Objective

By now, you should already know what your objective would be. We covered this in the section about presentation goals. Think about your presentation and develop a goal or objective for it:

- By the end of this presentation, the audience will understand the four dichotomies of the Myers-Briggs Type Indicator ®
- The goal of this presentation is to build a case for additional funding for the PTA
- My objective is to convince the group that The Rock is the greatest wrestler of all time

If you get the objective developed, the remaining steps should be fairly easy.

As long as your objective is achievable, and in some cases measurable, the rest of the process should go rather easily.

The Introduction – Telling Them What You're Going to Tell Them

Next to the objective, the introduction is the most important part of the presentation. The introduction sets the stage for the rest of the presentation. Additionally, it accomplishes the following:

You Capture the Listener's Attention

Depending on the setting, your audience may not be completely focused on your presentation. This is particularly true if you have to present first thing in the morning or shortly after lunch. If you begin with the body of your presentation without a strong introduction, they may not have an idea where you want to take them and might miss some very important information early on.

You Give the Audience a Reason to Listen

A strong introduction gets your audience's attention and builds the case for why your material is unique and important. Without the introduction, they may not grasp who YOU are and why YOUR material is worth listening to.

You Set the Proper Tone for the Topic and Setting

Regardless of your topic, proper tone helps an audience decide which "ear" to listen with. If your presentation is designed to be serious, they need to know before you get into the material. If it's of a lighthearted nature, they probably need to know it's ok to laugh now and then. The introduction gives them clear direction on the tone and setting so they can prepare accordingly.

You Establish Your Qualifications

Earlier in the book, we mentioned that in most cases, you are asked to speak because you are an expert. Your audience probably assumes that, and so for the sake of the theorists who may be in attendance, an introduction is your chance to state your qualifications. Maximizing your credibility is crucial – we'll cover that shortly.

You Introduce Your Objective and Preview the Presentation

For the sake of your pragmatist and reflector friends, it's always a good idea to open with an overview of what you're going to cover. You may also want to begin with a statement addressing the length of the presentation as well:

"For the next 40 minutes, I want to build the case for additional PTA funding."

Most people like to know how long you'll be presenting – and will let you know when your time is nearly up. We'll cover these non-verbal indicators later.

How do you deliver a strong introduction? It's quite important, but fortunately you have many choices when opening a presentation. Take a look at the following suggestions for some opening statements.

The introduction is your one and only chance to grab the audience's attention, so it's important to do it right. Take a look at the following strategies and see which ones appeal to you, and which ones you can comfortably and effectively open with.

Asking a Question

The late Andy Rooney of the TV show *60 Minutes* began most of his commentaries with a question:

"Have you ever wondered they lock the bathrooms at the gas station? What, are they afraid someone is going to break in and clean it?"

His purpose was to get us focused and thinking about his topic. Much of what he commented on seemed trivial, but with an opening question, it actually makes us take a second to consider, and by then he's already moving through his material and we decide to listen in.

Telling a Story

Storytelling is becoming a study and art of its own. Organizations use storytelling to convey the history and values it cherishes. Parents do it as a way to impart family traditions.

In an introduction, storytelling is a way to draw the audience in and grab their attention. Be sure your story is short, relevant, and non-controversial. It won't help if your story either puts the audience to sleep or causes them to leave the room.

Giving a Quotation

Reflectors and pragmatists love quotations. A good quotation can intrigue the audience, affirm your argument in advance, or help them connect the topic to something they believe in. Quotations from experts in your particular industry or organization are helpful too.

Some examples are:

"A wise man once said, if you always do what you've always done, you'll always get what you've always got." (and then follow with

a statement about the change you are trying to persuade the audience for)

"I remember kind of picking my head up from the mat and saying to the referee 'Tell him not to touch me, I can't move'." (and then make the case that while professional wrestling is entertainment, serious injuries can occur)

Be sure when appropriate to cite your source and also make sure you state the quote correctly and source correctly.

Making a Startling Statement

I began this book with a startling statement:

Speaking in front of a crowd scares me. Before each speech I give, workshop I facilitate, or class I teach, I say a silent prayer of hope that nobody shows up.

My whole point was to get your attention, and since you're still reading now, I guess it worked.

Startling statements are most effective when they relate directly to the topic. Take a look at the following:

"I believe that by the year 2025, we won't have smart phones, instead, people will have their devices embedded into their brain" (and then make the case for increased use of

segmentation for marketing your company's product)

"By the time I finish this presentation, 20 people will have died because of lung cancer" (and then make the case for a smoking cessation program at your organization)

Startling statements can shock your audience to attention. Using a strategically placed "pause" helps too. Just be sure your facts are correct in case your Theorists know what the real statistics are.

Referring to the Audience

Audiences pay better attention when they know the presentation is designed for them. It's the same reason we relate better to people who remember our name or something about us.

Referring to the audience can be as simple as just acknowledging they are in the room. You might say something like:

"It seems like just yesterday all of you were here listening to me drone on and on about the budget. Well as a result of your enduring that speech, I have some wonderful news to share about the results of your efforts."

"Every time I get asked to attend a presentation from a motivational speaker, I always wonder what we are doing wrong. Well, let me put your fears to rest by assuring

you that we are here to celebrate your achievements"

The eternal question for an audience is "What's in it for me?" Referring to them in the introduction answers that question and ensures they stay with you until the end.

Referring to the Occasion

Sometimes the occasion is obvious, but by referring to the occasion in the introduction, you appear to understand and know the audience. If you've been asked to speak for somebody else's organization, referring to the occasion lets the crowd see that you care enough to know a little about them.

Start with a statement such as:

"I'm pleased and honored to speak to you on this momentous occasion, the 25th anniversary of your merger with XYZ Corporation"

"Taking a risk with a new product is a scary prospect. You defied the odds, and now, at the 10 year celebration of your company, let me tell you how honored I am to celebrate with you."

Be gracious, be honest, and most of all, be sincere. Your audience will see right through you if you're not.

Using Humor

"An effective way to connect with your audience is to use humor. Don't be afraid to make yourself the object of a humorous story... mildly self-deprecating humor is disarming. Also, choose language that is easily understandable. Your goal is not to impress but to communicate! This does not mean talking down to your audience, but instead including them by defining any terms that may be technical or unfamiliar to them. If your audience feels comfortable with you rather than intimidated by you, they are more likely to get the most from your presentation, and you will have accomplished your goal."

Georgia Riojas Riverside, CA

Used correctly, humor is a powerful connector. As Georgia (who happened to be my 12th grade creative writing and speech teacher) mentioned above, humor is disarming, which is helpful if you're concerned about a hostile audience, and it makes the audience feel comfortable. Either way, you'll be more effective at getting your point across to them.

However, humor used incorrectly, specifically if done through joke telling, can destroy not only your presentation, but your credibility as well.

In workshops, I'm often asked what an appropriate joke might be. My answer is that no matter what the joke is, there is always the chance you'll offend somebody.

Question: "What's black and white and red all over?

Answer: "A skunk with diaper rash."

Could that joke offend somebody? Of course, it could be parents of infants, animal lovers, or anyone who may not share that sense of humor. My point is always the same: If a joke even has a remote chance of offending, are you willing to take the risk to tell it? And even if it doesn't offend, is it really the best way to kick off a presentation?

It's better to use a humorous story that ties directly to the topic. For example, if you were doing a presentation on filling out tax forms correctly and ethically, it may be appropriate to share the story of someone who tried to list their goldfish as a dependent. If you're speaking to a group and are the expert in your field, try telling a funny story about when you made a major mistake (assuming you think it's funny and aren't still suffering the consequences).

Enough can go wrong during a presentation. Do yourself a favor and use humor appropriately and sparingly – save the jokes for Impromptu Night at the local comedy club. It's customary to offend your audience there.

Points to Ponder

1. Am I confident enough about my objective to build my presentation on it?

2. Which of the introductory statements or strategies am I most comfortable using?

3. Is humor appropriate with the group I'll be speaking to?

What Else Can I Do To Make A Great Introduction?

Maximize your credibility. Think about it. Your audience wants to hear from an expert. You must be an expert if you were asked to speak. The task now becomes to show the audience your credentials without having to refer them to your biography. Here are some suggestions:

Demonstrate Your Competence

You must be at least a little competent if you were asked to speak. It's up to you to show the audience why you were chosen. Perhaps you might mention research you've done or certifications you've achieved. Maybe your position in the organization is one that through title alone sets you apart as an expert.

But people want to see results. It might be helpful to list achievements or results. The person introducing you can let the audience know this so it won't appear as if you're bragging. Having some of your publications handy will work – maybe you can refer them to a website or mention your article in a recent periodical. Be sure to do it humbly, yet confidently.

Earn the Trust of Your Audience

Trust is difficult to gain and easy to lose. Typically, trust is based on values. We spent some time talking about values and attitudes earlier – you may want to re-read that portion.

People will trust you if you give them enough reason to. Perhaps you might relay an incident or example of something trustworthy you've done in your field. If you can't think of one, relay the story of somebody else the audience knows and relates to, then affirm that story by showing your particular agreement with that person. By identifying credibly with trustworthy people, you can reap the benefit of that same trust.

Don't break this trust. If, after the presentation, you're caught doing the opposite of what you talked about, that and any subsequent presentations will be forever be tarnished.

Emphasize Your Similarity to the Audience

Opposites may attract, but similarities hold us together over time. Audiences are more interested in how well you relate to them in order for them to believe what you're telling them will actually work.

There are several ways to do this. Take a look at the following examples:

"Wow, I guess I'm the last speaker of the day. Can one of you keep an eye on the time for me? There's nothing worse than getting stuck in

rush hour traffic and I'll be on the beltway right behind you."

"I don't know about all of you, but I'm sure looking forward to lunch. As the last speaker before lunch, I'll be sure we finish on time so we all have plenty of time to eat."

"Wow, is anyone's backside as sore as mine? Sitting in presentations can really drain your energy. I promise to make my remarks brief and to the point."

Can an audience identify with that? Of course! We all get hungry, antsy, sore, and tired. The speaker merely affirms what they are all saying in their heads:

"Oh no, I hope he doesn't run us late – the traffic is horrible around here."

"Gosh I'm hungry – sure hope she doesn't run us into our lunch hour."

"My butt is sore – I wish we could take a stretch break – I hope he talks fast!"

Be a friend to your audience and show your similarities. It's ok to be human, even if you are the expert!

Increase Your Appeal to the Audience

Everything above will help you appeal to the audience, but there are five additional ways you can increase your favorability with them:

1. **Demonstrate Self-awareness** – this is exhibited by self-confidence, a realistic self-assessment, and a self-deprecating sense of humor.

2. **Demonstrate Self-management** – You'll see this in a speaker's trustworthiness, integrity, optimism, and organizational commitment.

3. **Demonstrate Self-motivation** – Those who defy the odds inspire people. Show your audience that you have a strong desire to achieve, are optimistic, and committed to the organization.

4. **Demonstrate Empathy** – Empathy is different than sympathy. A sympathetic statement might be, "gee, I'm sorry." An empathetic statement would be, "that's terrible – can I do anything to help?"

5. **Demonstrate Social Skills** – Social skills are nothing more than mastering verbal and non-verbal communication. This enhances your ability to be persuasive, and to build coalitions around commitment.

Are all of these possible to demonstrate during the introduction alone? I believe they are! We communicate so much through non-verbal language. Each of the above can be demonstrated through facial expression, tone of voice, eye contact, and a host of other methods. Your audience is sharp – they'll be able to spot it so work on these non-verbal parts of your presentation as well.

Demonstrate Sincerity

In America, we suffer from an epidemic of over-flattery. If you work in politics, entertainment, or really most other fields, the facades abound. It's difficult to find the sincerity in the syrup.

Your audience wants sincerity. Don't start off by telling them they are the best audience you've ever spoke to – they won't believe you, particularly if you've used that line before and somebody in the audience heard it.

Sincerity means that you're not perfect and don't claim to be. It means that you'll share stories of when you failed. You'll communicate it when you identify and empathize with them. Sincerity will cause the audience to overlook mistakes in your presentation. In a world of fluff, we are all searching for reality.

Wow, can you believe everything we just talked about was just for the introduction? The introduction is crucial. If you get it right, the presentation will flow smoothly. If you goof it up, you may never recover. Be sure to spend some time planning your introduction.

Points to Ponder

1. Am I credible?

2. What can I do personally to increase my credibility?

3. What common experiences do I share with my audience?

4. In what ways can I ensure the audience believes in me?

After finishing the objective and introduction, you need to think about organizing the body of your presentation.

The Body – Tell Them What You Want To Tell Them

After figuring out the objective and designing a strong introduction, it's time to give them the information. Using our earlier saying, this is where you tell them.

Your presentation body is made up of one or more points, with supporting information to follow. Each main point can be a different focus for you, and is a logical point in the presentation for a transition.

By keeping a focused, step-by-step outline, you'll have an easier time organizing your material, creating your handouts, and arranging your visual aids. Just use any outline format you're comfortable with. Don't be afraid to start with a big, detailed one. This is how you'll plan the entire body so you can fine-tune later.

We'll revisit the body of the presentation when we look at planning visual aids. But let's take a moment to take a look at communicating within the body of the presentation.

You told them what you were going to tell them, NOW TELL THEM!

Working the Body – The Informative Presentation

Let's begin our discussion of the body by focusing on the informative presentation. Remember, informative presentations are designed to share information. The information here also works when teaching and training. Remember, in that type of presentation, you're goal is to inform specifically, with action to follow.

When presenting to inform, brevity and clarity are key. Style is important, but not at the expense of substance. Here are four helpful hints when doing an informative presentation.

Cover Only Necessary Information

Think back to our discussion of personality types. We mentioned the function of information gathering and how a preference for Sensing necessitated a "here and now" approach while iNtuition enjoys a discussion of the contributing factors and other possibilities. You'll need to decide how much information is necessary in order to satisfy both. Remember, the informative presentation doesn't have to convince or persuade, so focus on what's necessary to make your point.

From a learning style perspective, remember that pragmatists and theorists need different information. This requires a balance between the theory and the practical. You'll have to look at the outline and decide which points need to be made so you won't bore part of the audience in order to reach the other parts.

Link the Topic to the Audience

When informing, be sure the audience has a reason to listen. Once again, asking the question, "what's in it for me?" from their perspective is helpful. Your pragmatists want to know how this topic can be applied, and the activists are already doing it in their mind, so be ready to address the impact of your subject right away.

Link the Unfamiliar to the Familiar

This is truly the secret to successful communication. Of course, you won't be able to do this if you haven't taken the time to know who your audience is. Can you see why knowing your audience before the presentation is so important?

If your goal is to inform, be sure your audience can relate to the topic. If the topic is totally new to them, try using techniques that will link what they don't know, to what they do know. Take a look at Stuart's suggestion:

"Use the power of metaphor to puzzle your audience and have them think about your topic. Search hard and creatively to find an example

that engages your audience by hooking them with something they recognize, but at the same time intrigues them with something unexplained.

At a meeting with a very diverse group meeting for the first time I was at a loss for a way to create a theme. I hit on the idea of 'weaving a blanket' that took their diverse experiences and backgrounds and compared them to threads woven together by their interaction at the meeting. Meeting and talking, sharing a common experience together at the meeting created a virtual "blanket" - surrounding everyone, keeping them warm, safe and secure and providing lasting value. Avoid tired examples like 'home runs', 'outside the box' and 'blocking and tackling.' Biology (and other sciences) provides a rich source, but seek out ideas from other cultures, history, anthropology and biographies etc. Old ways of thinking can be shaken up by freshness from an unfamiliar parallel.

Make your metaphor come to life, by rehearsing - not using a detailed script - but with cue cards that have "bullets" to lay out the structure of your ideas. Each bullet is a paragraph that you have internalized."

Stuart Wilkinson, Memphis, TN

Having listened to many of Stuart's presentations (he was my old Boss back in 1999), I can tell you his use of the metaphor is very effective. Take a look at the next example from the Bible.

While Paul was waiting for them in Athens, he was greatly distressed to see that the city was full of idols.

So he reasoned in the synagogue with the Jews and the God-fearing Greeks, as well as in the marketplace day by day with those who happened to be there.

A group of Epicurean and Stoic philosophers began to dispute with him. Some of them asked, "What is this babbler trying to say?" Others remarked, "He seems to be advocating foreign gods." They said this because Paul was preaching the good news about Jesus and the Resurrection.

Then they took him and brought him to a meeting of the Areopagus, where they said to him, "May we know what this new teaching is that you are presenting?

You are bringing some strange ideas to our ears, and we want to know what they mean."

(All the Athenians and the foreigners who lived there spent their time doing nothing but talking about and listening to the latest ideas.)

Paul then stood up in the meeting of the

Areopagus and said: "Men of Athens! I see that in every way you are very religious.

For as I walked around and looked carefully at your objects of worship, I even found an altar with this inscription: TO AN UNKNOWN GOD. Now what you worship as something unknown I am going to proclaim to you.

Acts 17:16-23

This is a great story and a wonderful example of linking unfamiliar to familiar. In this story, Paul is trying to get his message across to the wise Greek philosophers. Talk about a difficult audience! Stoics were concerned with getting meaning from life through minimalism and living without pleasure, while Epicureans advocated pleasure over all else. Neither audience would have related to Paul's message of the Gospel as it was typically preached, so he does it by reaching them on their level. Paul appears to think well on his feet doesn't he? I think it's a great strategy, referencing their unknown god. If something is unknown, and you appear to know about it, you're automatically the expert. Greek philosophers obviously valued the opinions of experts.

Was he successful? Take a look:

When they heard about the resurrection of the dead, some of them sneered, but others said, "We want to hear you again on this subject.

At that, Paul left the Council.

A few men became followers of Paul and believed. Among them was Dionysius, a member of the Areopagus, also a woman named Damaris, and a number of others.

Looks like it worked! Do you think the Greek philosophers would have listened to his regular sermon and understood? Probably not. And remember, some of the philosophers wanted to hear him speak again. It's always nice to be asked back by your audience.

How can you learn to come up with creative stories and metaphors? It may come natural to iNtuitive personalities, but for others it takes work. Consider practicing your presentation in front of several diverse groups and ask for their feedback and ideas. You might also want to do some reading, not just textbooks, but maybe some poetry or fiction. Pay attention to the author's style and the way they use words. You might get some very unique and effective ideas for use in your own presentation.

Involve the Audience

Involving the audience to participate in the presentation is another way to ensure the information sinks in. Remember, you activists are already doing it, and the pragmatists are just itching to see how your information really works. Try a few of the following suggestions to get your audience involved:

- Case studies
- Problem solving
- Brainstorming
- Discussions
- Role playing
- Discussions

The location and venue may not make this possible, but when you can, try to provide at least one activity that meets the needs of your activists and pragmatists.

Working the Body – The Persuasive Presentation

Persuasive presentations work a little differently than informative. Persuasive presentations serve to convince your audience of something and get them moving forward on it.

Your goal in a persuasive presentation is to mobilize and move the audience forward. It's designed to convince them that your points are valid and they should rush to comply. You may do a little informing, but ultimately, the goal is to move the audience to action. Providing information alone, even if you use creative metaphors and stories, won't necessarily cause the group to take action.

Here are some strategies for an effective persuasive presentation:

Appeal to the Needs of the Audience

In 1954, Abraham Maslow reasoned that human beings go through life in a quest to satisfy needs. He listed five of them in the hierarchy.

1. **Physiological** – hunger, thirst, shelter, sex

2. **Safety** – security and protection from physical and emotional harm

3. **Love** – affection, belongingness, acceptance, and friendship

4. **Esteem** – internal esteem factors such as self- respect, autonomy, and achievement as well as external factors such as status, recognition, and attention

5. **Self-actualization** – the drive to become what we are capable of (growth, achieving potential, self- fulfillment)

As humans achieve satisfaction at one level, the goal becomes realizing the next level. Sometimes though, a lower order need may re-emerge, throwing off the entire sequence. Let's say for example that I have achieved the Esteem level. I'm a Vice President of a large department, have the great pay, benefits, and respect as well as all the perquisites such as a parking space, key to the executive bathroom, etc. Then one day I lose my job. This pushes me all the way down the pyramid as I struggle to not only re-achieve my esteem needs, but even the more lower order needs such as paying the mortgage. Suddenly, that close parking space and fancy bathroom doesn't mean quite as much! My immediate goal becomes one of survival.

So how does impact you as a presenter? If you're doing a persuasive presentation, try to gauge what specific needs your audience has. Your goal is to convince them of something; tie it into one of Maslow's levels. If the presentation is supposed to convince them a change in HR policy is good, link it to perhaps their safety and security need. For presentations that focus on new opportunities or challenges, perhaps you can tie it into achieving esteem or self- actualization needs. Remember, if Maslow is correct, than everyone, including you, is on a quest to achieve self-actualization. Consider their needs as you develop your persuasive strategy.

Have a Realistic Goal

Dreaming is a great thing! Setting incredible goals and achieving them is even better. Nobody should tell you to think small and think realistically. When giving a persuasive presentation however, being realistic is important.

Having a realistic goal in a persuasive presentation means that what you set out to achieve is actually achievable. It may not happen immediately, but at least the audience has all the facts, and enough motivation to get started.

Convincing an audience is no easy task. Even the Apostle Paul in the earlier example didn't convert all the Greek philosophers, but that didn't keep him from trying. He also didn't leave the Areopagus angry and discouraged. His goal was realistic – to present the material the best way he could and celebrate the result, regardless of the outcome. Martin Luther King, Jr. didn't find civil rights immediately improved when he stepped down from Lincoln Memorial in 1963, but the momentum was started.

We can learn much from these examples. Dream big – but realize that big dreams are achieved at times with "baby steps." Prepare to inform and motivate your audience, but understand that initial actions may be small and sometimes unnoticeable. A realistic goal is to just get the process moving.

Defer the Thesis with a Hostile Audience

Not every audience will be excited to hear from you. In fact, they might even know exactly what you're going to present, and planning to listen with a closed mind. All the preparation with personality awareness, learning style, etc. won't prevent pre-conceived notions from appearing.

Does this means you should fake an illness and not show up? Of course not! You'll just need to change your tactics. In our outline, we said to tell the audience what we're going to tell them, tell them, then tell them what we just told them. With a hostile audience, it's best not to tell them what you're going to tell them. After all, they probably know it anyway. Defer that statement until later, or don't use it at all. What does this mean?

If an audience is hostile or potentially hostile, you can bet it's because something is going to be changed for them. People are usually reluctant to change, even if it's for something better. Your job is to convince them the change is good. Remember our discussion of Maslow and the needs. You might want to try addressing those needs, and then subtly introduce the change as meeting or acknowledging the need. Your goal is to take the hostile energy from the audience otherwise they won't listen anyway. Use a good introduction with a story or quote; disarm them through some interesting facts or figures. When the initial adrenaline is expended from the audience, you'll have a much easier time getting your information out. Defer or eliminate divulging your thesis with a hostile audience.

Present Ample Information to Support Your Claims

All adult learners want information. They may each process it differently, but statements without information won't convince them of anything.

Your information may come in the form of visuals, handouts, references, or through your verbal presentation. Be sure you have facts and figures to back up each of your claims. A statement of greatness becomes just another opinion without some data to prove it.

We'll revisit this when we talk later about effective visual aids.

Consider Citing Opposing Ideas

Again, your audience isn't stupid. If your topic is controversial, they probably have lots of data to refute it. Why not take away their momentum by citing that very data? It will give you instant credibility for several reasons.

First, you'll appear to be extremely prepared. Anyone can gather enough information to support their own claims, but it's impressive to see someone that took the time to get the opposing data as well.

Secondly, you'll appear to be objective. Objective people look at all sides of an issue with an open mind. By addressing the opposing views, you'll show the audience that you've weighed the facts and figures and know what you're talking about.

Finally, you'll appear courageous. People are attracted to those who face adversity head on. If you address opposing views, the audience sees that you don't run from danger and are capable of handling it.

Always prepare for an audience that knows more than you do. Good preparation, studying all sides of the issue, will give you a very strong chance of convincing them.

Adapt to the Cultural Style of the Audience

Human nature tells us to like what we know and understand. When it comes to people, we are most comfortable dealing with people who are like us.

In 1996, I attended a concert at a county fair in Puyallup, Washington. The headliner was country music star John Michael Montgomery and there were two preliminary performers, one of which was an established group with significant airplay, Ricochet, and a newcomer named Kevin Sharpe. Kevin Sharpe came out dressed in a Seattle Mariners baseball jersey and completely appealed to the Washington crowd in every way. He referenced their weather, their culture, and their sports teams – essentially making Washington HIS home state. The crowd loved it and him. He played several encores and nobody wanted him to leave.

When Ricochet followed him, the energy was gone. There was no local appeal, just the feeling that this group was a bigger star and we were privileged to listen to them. In fact, when they finished and left the stage, there was no chant for an encore, but the band reappeared in about a minute as if there was a call for one. It was the strangest thing I had ever seen at a concert and a constant reminder how important it is to acknowledge and appreciate an audience. Adapting to their cultural style is very important.

How can you do it? Again, do your research. Find out what your audience is interested in. Do some research on the dress code and other cultural issues. Find out what the buzzwords are. Ask beforehand what major issues this group has faced. Figure out what their hot buttons are so you don't push them.

Final Thoughts on the Presentation Body

The body makes up the bulk of your presentation. Your introduction opens the door, but the information in the body is really what the audience comes for. Be sure the body is thorough, concise, addresses all the points, and is deliverable in the amount of time allotted. Your visual aids, if any, will be most effective here.

Once you've delivered the material, only one step remains – the conclusion!

The Conclusion – Telling Them What You Just Told Them

It's almost over! You've developed a strong objective, started off with a great introduction, and organized a structured, well-thought out body. All that's left is to wrap it up and go home.

The conclusion is your opportunity to make a lasting final impression with your audience. It's a way to wrap up your material in a neat package with a fancy ribbon. A weak conclusion waters down your message. No conclusion leaves an audience feeling uncertain and wondering what happens next.

The Transition

As important as the conclusion itself is the transition to the conclusion. People like to know when it's safe to close their note and look at their watches. Hopefully, if you told them in the introduction...

"For the next 20 minutes, I'd like to convince you that The Rock is the greatest wrestler of all time"

...you actually stuck to that time frame. Your audience will hold you to your word, and punish you with negative body language if you fail to live up to it.

It's helpful to let them know the end is near. Here are some suggestions:

- *"And in conclusion..."*
- *"Finally, let me say that..."*
- *"As we wrap up this presentation, let me say..."*

Be sure to practice this transition! Too much formality makes it sound fake, too little may cause the audience to miss it.

Once the transition is made, it's time to wrap it up and hit the road. Here are some good ways to conclude your presentation:

Give a Review

We said earlier the conclusion was telling the audience what you just told them. You could conclude by doing a quick review of the body. The conclusion in our sample outline gives a nice framework:

"Because of his career history, achievements, quality of opponents, and his influence in the sport, I submit that The Rock Is The Greatest Wrestler Of All Time"

You could BRIEFLY reiterate a little about each point, but this is to serve only as a reminder. If the presentation itself was short, be sure the conclusion is as well. If you presented for over an hour, you could lengthen your conclusion accordingly.

Use Something Similar to the Opening

Following the theme of your presentation is a great idea. If your opening statement was a story or a quotation, you might want to end it similarly. If you used a shocking statement, it might be helpful to repeat the statement, and make it sound far less shocking because of the material you presented.

Continuity is a trademark of good presenters. It makes you look as though you thought out your material and practiced it. It also helps your transition look even smoother. If your introduction was well built, the conclusion is a natural bookend. Mirror it for excellent results.

Return to the Theme of the Opening Statement

This is similar to the previous point, but focusing on the theme means considering the audience and occasion as well. If it's a celebratory event, finish with acknowledgement of that. If it's a big change in structure or procedure, revisit that.

Appeal for Action

This is the cornerstone of a persuasive presentation. After all, this is what you want the audience to hear: what do we do now?

Take a look at the following example from John F. Kennedy's inauguration speech on January 20, 1961:

"Can we forge against these enemies a grand and global alliance, north and south, east and west, that can assure a more fruitful life for all mankind? Will you join in that historic effort?

In the long history of the world, only a few generations have been granted the role of defending freedom in its hour of maximum danger. I do not shrink from this responsibility-I welcome it. I do not believe that any of us would exchange places with any other people or any other generation. The energy, the faith, the devotion which we bring to this endeavor will light our country and all who serve it-and the glow from that fire can truly light the world.

And so, my fellow Americans: ask not what your country can do for you- ask what you can do for your country.

My fellow citizens of the world: ask not what America will do for you, but what together we can do for the freedom of man.

Finally, whether you are citizens of America or citizens of the world, ask of us here the same high standards of strength and sacrifice which we ask of you. With a good conscience our only sure reward, with history the final judge of our deeds, let us go forth to lead the land we love, asking His blessing and His help, but knowing that here on earth God's work must truly be our own."

What was Kennedy's appeal to action? It was for us as Americans to take action and serve our country. The body of his speech laid out some very scary scenarios that were currently playing out in the world. He carried an ominous message, but also sprinkled it with hope. The body contained a very famous line:

"All this will not be finished in the first 100 days. Nor will it be finished in the first 1,000 days, not in the life of this Administration, nor even perhaps in our lifetime on this planet. But let us begin."

His conclusion brought the thoughts to a close. Our challenge was to consider the issues in the world and make a decision to take action rather than sit back and watch it happen. It was a very powerful speech and is a fine example of a call to action in the conclusion.

End with a Challenge

Ending with a challenge is similar to the appeal for action. Again, it's a natural conclusion for a persuasive speech. There may not be specific action required, but this should give an audience powerful thoughts to consider. Let's take another look at Martin Luther King, Jr.'s I have a dream speech:

"With this faith we will be able to work together, to pray together, to struggle together, to go to jail together, to stand up for freedom together, knowing that we will be free one day.

This will be the day when all of God's children will be able to sing with a new meaning, "My country, 'tis of thee, sweet land of liberty, of thee I sing. Land where my fathers died, land of the pilgrim's pride, from every mountainside, let freedom ring." And if America is to be a great nation, this must become true. So let freedom ring from the prodigious hilltops of New Hampshire.

Let freedom ring from the mighty mountains of New York. Let freedom ring from the heightening Alleghenies of Pennsylvania! Let freedom ring from the snowcapped Rockies of Colorado! Let freedom ring from the curvaceous peaks of California! But not only that; let freedom ring from Stone Mountain of Georgia! Let freedom ring from Lookout Mountain of Tennessee! Let freedom ring from every hill and every molehill of Mississippi. From every mountainside, let freedom ring.

When we let freedom ring, when we let it ring from every village and every hamlet, from every state and every city, we will be able to speed up that day when all of God's children, black men and white men, Jews and Gentiles, Protestants and Catholics, will be able to join hands and sing in the words of the old Negro spiritual, "Free at last! free at last! thank God Almighty, we are free at last!"

Certainly Martin Luther King, Jr. could have given a 10-point action plan, but at the time, there appeared to be little hope for African Americans. Instead, he chose to have the audience experience HIS dream. His challenge was for all of us to visualize an incredible future, and take small steps to make it happen.

And In Conclusion...

Don't skimp on the conclusion. Think about the most powerful speeches in history. Can you imagine Martin Luther King, Jr. cutting off his I have a dream speech without its famous "Free at Last" ending? How about Ronald Reagan issuing his challenge against Communism without imploring Mikhail Gorbechav to *"Tear down this Wall!"* A strong presentation with a weak conclusion translates into a weak presentation.

A Final Word About Planning Your Outline

We jumped around a little in this chapter. We started by talking about how to write an outline, but then gave you lots of tips and techniques to actually give the presentation. I did this intentionally.

Planning your outline means planning out your entire speech. The outline is really your cheat sheet. It should be what guides you in making your points. An outline without action leads to a boring, methodical presentation that will hypnotize your audience.

As you plan your outline, mentally put yourself in front of the audience and give the presentation. Remember the visualization we did earlier. See it in your mind and the audience will see it with their eyes and hear it with their ears!

Points to Ponder

1. Are my thoughts organized enough to begin my outline?

2. Have I spent enough time visualizing my presentation as a product of total perfection?

3. Do I know my audience well enough to tailor an introduction to them?

4. Does my conclusion give the presentation enough energy and leave the audience feeling challenged?

Planning Your Visual Aids

It may seem odd to talk about visual aids at the very end of the planning section, but I did it for a specific reason. Most folks spend a lot of time developing incredible visual aids. In many cases, the visuals are planned before the presentation itself! We'll talk more about that ill-advised procedure later, but for now let's focus on the different options available.

Visuals are an important part of a presentation. They provide clarity, add a degree of interest, and in many cases serve are part of the entertainment feature of presentations. When we think about the learning styles of our audiences, we know that the Theorists probably expect some type of visuals, and the Activists like to see them for reference as they explore the topic as well. Visuals may consist of one or more of the following:

Electronic (PowerPoint®)

This is the most common of all the visuals. PowerPoint® presentations are convenient and relatively inexpensive. It's easy to use and contains everything you need to combine text, colors, photos, graphics, and video into a nice presentation, complete with customized handouts.

It's rare to attend any presentation that doesn't include some electronic component. Most presenters today are trained with electronics, and some college courses require the use of this type of visual for student presentations.

However all of this leads to several problems.

Over Dependency

When used well, PowerPoint® enhances a presentation and gives it a sense of quality and excellence. But PowerPoint®'s use creates a dependence that's hard to break.

Once of the best things that ever happened to me was getting a job at a company that didn't have a multimedia projector. I was so used to teaching classes and giving presentations in the Navy using PowerPoint®, that for a moment I didn't know if I could teach without it. Thankfully I was forced to break my PowerPoint® addiction!

Think of the most power speeches given in history. Would Lincoln's Gettysburg Address made more of an impact with animated bullet points screeching in from the right side of the slide? Would *I Have A Dream* been more inspiring with streaming video and brilliantly choreographed slide transitions? Absolutely not!

Design Flaws

Access to a canvas and brushes won't automatically make you an artist. PowerPoint® contains lots of neat features, colors, animations, and ideas, but none of these will help you if the design is bad.

Designing your slides can be easy if you make one critical distinction: are the slides for my use or for the audience to see?

If the slides are for you, then design them to be idea-prompters. If they are for the audience, then make them short and self-explanatory. If you're careful, you can accomplish both. The slide on the previous pages is a great example of a prompter for the speaker and a nice "roadmap" for an audience.

On the next several pages, you'll see some examples of what I refer to as the "Good, the Bad, and the Ugly!"

> For sexual harassment to occur, unwelcome sexual behavior must occur in or impact on the work environment:
>
> When recipients are offered or denied something that is work-connected in return for submitting to or rejecting unwelcome sexual behavior, they have been subjected to a type of sexual harassment known as :quid pro quo: ("this for that"). Examples include: getting or losing a job, a promotion or demotion, a good or bad performance evaluation, etc. Basically if any work-connected decisions are made based on the submission to or rejection of the unwelcome sexual behavior, sexual harassment has occurred. Normally, this is from a senior to a junior, because the senior person has something to offer.

The Good

Good material. Lots of information.

The Bad

Too much information for one slide. It could be used more effectively as a handout.

The Ugly

This slide is way too busy and the text is too small – using a sans serif (without the little "feet" on the letters) is a better choice.

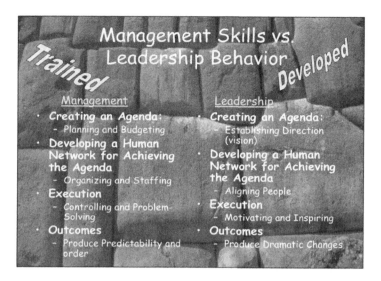

The Good

Good material. Lots of information.

The Bad

Too much information for one slide. Font sizes are disproportionate.

The Ugly

Who chose that background? Ouch!

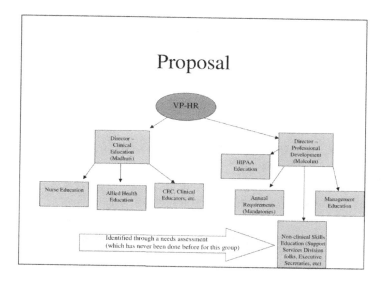

The Good

Good choice of use. Flowcharts work well on PowerPoint®.

The Bad

Boxes are too small – might be better to break it up into several smaller charts.

The Ugly

Text should be uniform in centering and spacing all boxes.

Open the Interview

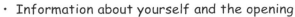

- Greeting
- Offer something to drink
- Idle "chit - chat"
- Information about yourself and the opening
- Time required for the interview
- The way the interview will be conducted
- Note-taking/recording process

The Good

Designed for both the presenter and the audience – just enough information for both.

The Bad

Never use the Comic Sans font. Unless your audience is kindergartners.

The Ugly

Not sure why the happy face is there.

"Patient Care is our First Concern"

How we care for patients:

- **Nearly 500 clinicians.**
- **800 support staff.**
- **Over 40 outpatient & hospital-based sites in Shelby, Tipton, DeSoto, Crittenden, and Madison counties.**
- **Over 100 sites in 150 mile radius of Memphis.**

The Good

Overall very good. Concise and makes its points clearly.

The Bad

Try making the body of this unbolded. The bold font doesn't add much and tends to unbalance the slide.

The Ugly

Nothing really.

Dealing with Stress

- Take a "Stress Audit"
- Get regular exercise
- Eat well
- Monitor personal health
- Learn to identify and reduce sources of stress

The Good

Nice balance of text – works for both presenter and audience.

The Bad

Dark background works OK as projected, but it may not make a clear handout

The Ugly

Nothing really – I'm not a huge fan of Times New Roman fonts, but it's just my preference.

Verble Support

- Examples
- Stories
- Statistics
- Comparisons
- Citations

The Good

Excellent information. Nice use of the bullet points.

The Bad

Take a look at the title. Take extra precautions to spell check your slides!!!!

The Ugly

All of it. A misspelled slide is the ultimate curse for a presentation.

Types of Presentations

- Informative
- Persuasive
- Teaching/Training

The Good

Concise, simple, and effective.

The Bad

What in the world is that graphic there for? Use clipart sparingly, and be sure it actually adds something to the slide. Actually, never use clipart. Use a photo if you need a visual.

The Ugly

All of it – that graphic just ruined it for me!

As you can see, it doesn't take much to ruin a slide. Be very careful when working through your designs. If possible, use a standard template in the PowerPoint® software. These templates have optimum font sizes as a default. If you type in more than will fit, fonts automatically adjust downward. If you find this happening, use it as a clue to make your text bullets shorter! Don't try to pack as much information on your slide as you can.

In choosing color, use a medium colored dark background for projection, and switch to black and white (a white background) when printing your slides for the handouts. Once again, use one of the more conservative templates available in PowerPoint® and don't customize it.

Many companies offer customized templates designed by experts. If you must use PowerPoint®, consult one of them to help you with designs. If your organization has a standard template and it contains flawed design components, suggest some changes using ideas from this book. Remember, the goal of the presentation is to communicate. If the visuals are a distraction, that goal won't be met.

Technical Difficulties

Technical difficulties are always a possibility. The more elaborate your presentation visuals, the greater the risk of having trouble. Here are just some of your potential problems:

- Laptop getting dropped on the way to the presentation
- Slide show files getting damaged
- Projector bulb burning out
- No power source on the stage
- No extension cord when you need it
- Computer or projector freezing up
- Remote control for slide changes not working
- No "slide monkey" to sit there and advance your slides for you

You can probably think of many more. This short list should make the next point imperative.

No Back Up Plan

Be sure to have an alternate plan. This includes carrying your presentation on a thumb drive and/or CD, bringing your own extension cord and power strip, taking along a copy of the presentation on paper, or any other crisis-preventing ideas you can think of. I have a bag with every possible adapter and cord I would need to hook up a Macbook. This accompanies me everywhere.

It may also help to learn how all your equipment works instead of relying on someone at the presentation to get it working for you.

Learn to be more comfortable advancing your own slides. Practice opening up the projector and changing a bulb. You'll look more competent and confident to the audience if you don't fumble around like a helpless moron when getting your presentation together.

Loss of Spontaneity and Creativity

Herein lies the greatest danger in using PowerPoint®. It comes from this common mistake:

Most presentations are designed specifically for use with PowerPoint® rather than working hard to develop a good presentation and then deciding how to best use PowerPoint® to present it.

I fell into this trap early in my training career and it took a long time to get out of it. You'll find yourself designing for the slide rather than the audience. The material loses its own impact and more importantly, your creativity and thumbprint.

I kicked away the PowerPoint® crutch by slowly limiting myself to fewer slides. Eventually, I managed to get myself down to one slide. Once I could do it with one, I realized I could do it with none. The freedom I experienced was incredible. There was no longer any anxiety when computers or projectors failed. More than that, it allowed me to put more of my SELF into the presentation and let the strength of the material win the audience.

Take back creative control of your presentation! Design it as if you only had your presence with no visuals. Use visuals sparingly. Your audience came to see you; the visuals are your tool, not your master. Use them, don't let them use you!

One last important tip that applies to all visuals:

NEVER READ YOUR SLIDES TO THE AUDIENCE!

It's the quickest way to make your audience feel stupid and they WILL resent it!

Charts and Graphs

Charts and graphs are extremely important to the Theorists. Remember, their learning style is all about getting the background and foreground of the subject. Additionally, the type of audience may dictate the use of charts and graphs. If you are speaking to accountants and engineers, charts and graphs are their language.

Charts and graphs are also helpful if you're explaining economic data and trends. Remember how Ross Perot used charts in his addresses to the American public during his Presidential campaign of 1992? His platform for the election weighed in heavily on fixing the economy and so he chose his visuals very wisely.

Be sure when using charts and graphs that you make them large enough to see and spend time explaining exactly what it is your trying to show. You may choose to show them using slides, transparencies, or electronically. It's also helpful to provide copies to your audience, either before or after the presentation. We'll talk about how to do that shortly.

Benefits:

Charts and graphs are a convenient and effective way to display graphically related data. They appeal to certain audiences depending on the topic.

Drawbacks:

Charts and graphs can be expensive to produce and difficult to see. You'll have to be sure the data is accurate and correctly displays the points you're trying to make. They can also be difficult to see and understand if not displayed correctly.

Best Used When:

Making presentations on   data-related subjects and with audiences that prefer seeing background information and statistics.

Flip Charts and Poster Board

Flip charts are a very handy tool when making presentations. They are manufactured in a number of different sizes, styles, and colors. You can purchase them with lines and with a self-adhesive strip across the back, which makes them easy to hang anywhere.

Flip charts can be pre-made or you can write out your points as you go. You can be very spontaneous with them and take them anywhere quite easily. I recommend keeping a set of the self-adhering Post It® flip charts in the trunk of your car and two or three colored markers as well. This way you always have visuals available if your venue doesn't.

Poster board is similar to flip charts but are normally developed professionally and matted on a hard foam backing. Done correctly, they are beautiful and can be used over and over again. Poster boards however can be expensive to develop and are hard to travel with. They have a tendency to bend over time and the corners quickly get chipped and bent if you use them often.

Benefits:

Flip charts are lightweight, flexible, inexpensive and convenient. You can prepare them ahead of time, or tailor them spontaneously to your audience Poster boards look nice and can be used multiple times.

Drawbacks:

If your handwriting is poor or you have difficulty spelling some words correctly, the flipchart may not be a good choice. Flipcharts may also be hard to read if your audience is large or doesn't have a clear view of the front of the room.

Poster boards can be expensive, difficult to travel with, and impossible to modify. Be sure you're data is static and correct before investing in poster board.

Best Used When:

Flipcharts: Speaking to small groups and when the presentation has to be tailored on the fly.

Poster boards: Speaking to many small groups with data that won't change.

Slides (yeah, real slides, not PowerPoint®)

Slides are photographs printed onto film that can be viewed on a large scale using a slide projector. Slides are popular, particularly in the medical community with presentations on certain diseases or conditions. You may also see them used in classes or presentations involving art or perhaps trips taken to foreign locations.

Slides are used less today because of the

use of digital photography and laptop computers and projectors. Slides are a little more expensive to produce and it's getting more difficult to find venues with slide projectors.

Benefits:

Photographs can look beautiful when magnified. A well-planned slide show can be entertaining and informative.

Drawbacks:

Slides can be cumbersome to load in carousels and it's increasingly harder to find slide projectors. If you opt for slide-like quality, get a digital camera or scan your photos and use a computer to display them.

Best Used When:

Speaking to a large audience with a topic that includes photographs.

Handouts

Handouts are any materials you give to your audience. They may be used in conjunction with all the other visuals we've talked about so far, or as a standalone resource.

When using handouts, you can either follow the format of your visuals, or give out a narrative summary. Your handouts can fill in all the details while your presentation covers the main points.

I recommend giving the handouts to the audience AFTER your presentation, unless you need them to follow along with you. They can be a distraction and sometimes even create confusion in your audience *("what page is that on?"* or, *"is this covered in the handouts? I don't see it!").*

The design of the handout is up to you. You can follow the outline, make copies of your transparencies and charts, or simply use the handout feature of PowerPoint®. Be sure to bring enough copies for each attendee or the buzz created from sharing the handouts may distract them or you.

Benefits:

Handouts are an effective way to get your message to the audience. Some learners process information better if they can refer to it later. Handouts also do away with the need to take a lot of notes. Your audience may be so focused on taking notes that they'll miss part of your presentation.

Drawbacks:

Handouts can be a distraction, expensive to produce, and difficult to carry and pass out.

Best Used When:

Making any presentation – in conjunction with all other visuals.

Points to Ponder

1. Did I make the right choice for visuals?

2. Am I comfortable enough with my choice of visuals to handle problems if they arise during the presentation?

3. Are my visuals designed for my audience or will they have trouble relating to them?

4. Am I a PowerPoint® "junkie?"

5. Do I have a strategy in place to kick away the PowerPoint ®crutch?

Your planning is done, now practice your presentation! Visualize and practice, visualize and practice, visualize and practice!

Preparation and practice put fear into submission!

Chapter 4
Execute

Everything we've covered to this point is planning and preparation. Using our boxing analogy, think of that time as being in training camp. Training camp is a place to condition, and strategize. You'll do plenty of roadwork and sparring. Perhaps you'll watch films of your opponent.

Eventually, you'll break camp and get to the venue where your fight will be held. By now, the training should have made everything about this fight automatic in your mind. If you trained properly, you'll almost be fighting on instinct!

Much of what you do in the short period between preparation and presentation has the potential to either ruin your hard work, or give you the final "polish" before you present. How you treat yourself during that final day before the presentation could make all the difference in a rousing success, or a less favorable result.

With that in mind, let's go over some techniques to prepare you for the main event!

Get Some Sleep

I know this is easier said than done. If you've been nervous thinking about this day, you'll probably be too wound up to sleep.

However a good night's sleep will leave you refreshed and with the ability to get through all your material and make all of your points clearly.

Here are a few suggestions for getting a restful night of sleep before the main event:

- Turn the TV off
- Turn your phone off
- Eat a light meal
- No caffeine (this means sodas and chocolate too!)
- No alcohol (yes, this means beer too!)
- No sleeping pills
- Take a hot bath
- Go for a long walk in the early evening

Everything you do the night before should be conflict and stress free. If you always get into arguments with certain people, don't visit or call them that evening. When you crawl into bed, don't do your visualization activities, even if they're totally positive (and they always should be). Relax and do something nice for yourself.

I often get up in the middle of the night before big events. When that happens, I usually start to think about the big event, which gets my mind working, then before I know it, I'll be wide awake and unable to wind back down and go to sleep. If this happens to you, just get up. Go to your living room, turn the light on, and read a book. You'll be amazed at how tired you'll get and before you know it, you'll get back to bed and fall asleep quickly. If you just can't seem to relax, get in the shower and get dressed. Your body will adapt to the early hour and you probably won't feel tired. If your event is later that evening, you can always take a nap.

Eat Light

Sometimes you'll be presenting at a lunch or dinner event. Usually, you'll do your speech either during dessert or shortly after. What you eat during that time is important.

Don't eat a huge meal. Your body requires energy to digest food. If you're stuffing yourself with a lot of heavy food, your circulatory system will be working overtime to get digestion going. You need that circulatory system to be flooding your brain!

Try eating fruit, salads or some light pasta. Save the steak and baked potato for your celebration dinner. Avoid spicy or very salty foods. You'll want to get in front of the crowd feeling your best, not worried about water retention or an upset stomach. Don't drink a lot of caffeine or alcohol. You don't want to approach the podium tipsy or with an overactive bladder. Also, don't drink any carbonated drinks before speaking. You don't want to be up there in front of everyone burping or getting the hiccups. These same rules apply for meals eaten the night before your presentation. Moderation and discretion are your friends here. Don't overdo it – feed your brain and it will be there for you the next day!

Don't Over Train

It's possible to be TOO prepared. Over training is a common problem with athletes. If you watch a lot of boxing, you'll hear commentators make remarks that the fighter "left the fight in the gym."

I've worked with enough presenters to see the results of over-preparation. There is a fine balance between knowing your material, and having it so memorized that it becomes flat and uninspiring. Practice is important, but when your coach or the people you work with tell you that *"you've got it,"* then begin to ramp down your preparation. Visualization is enough practice for you at this point.

Visualize Nothing But Positive

This is nothing more than a reminder. Visualize perfection and you can't help but hit excellence. Refuse to think any negative thoughts. If your preparation was thorough, you'll do just fine!

Double Check Your Visuals

Your visuals of course should be irrelevant. In other words, people are coming to hear YOU speak, not to see your visuals. However if you're going to use them, do one last check to ensure they're ready as well. Make sure your markers are in your bag if you're using a flip chart. Double check the version of your PowerPoint® slides and make sure the draft you're using is the right one. If you're bringing your own laptop and projector, gather up all the cords, adapters, manuals, recovery disks, and extra bulbs and put them in your car. Make a checklist if that helps. The preparation has paid off – now it's time to tap into your inner strength and deliver the knockout!

The moments before your big event could be very tense. If you feel your heart racing and your breathing labored, this is normal! Remember the difference between fear and adrenaline? If you've prepared well, fear should not exist. Then our goal is to temper the adrenaline so we don't get up in front of the audience and finish our 30-minute presentation in five minutes. Try the following techniques to calm yourself down:

Breathe

Correct breathing is key to relaxing and ridding our bodies of toxins and stress. When we inhale, air enters the lungs and eventually makes its way to the cells via the blood stream. When we exhale, we rid the body of carbon dioxide and negative thoughts. Ironically, when we become stressed, we breathe faster and use only 1/3 of our lung capacity. This decrease in oxygen increases stress by contributing to lethargy (increased tiredness), preventing the release of toxins and increasing the workload of other body systems (especially the respiratory, cardiovascular, and nervous system).

Breathing is so automatic that most of us are not aware of how we breathe. Deep breathing (abdominal breathing) is the proper way to breathe. Place your hand on your lower stomach. Your hand should move outward (not your chest) as you inhale. Breathe in as deeply as possible, hold it, and breathe out slowly. Making this a daily practice during non-stressful situations will make this tool available to you during stressful times.

Smile

It takes more facial muscles to frown than it does to smile. Relax your face and the rest of your body by smiling. You'll feel better about yourself and your audience will get the idea that you're friendly and happy to be there.

Think Happy Thoughts

As part of your visualization, you should be incorporating the feelings you felt during happy times in your life. Anchor yourself to these good memories and take in the positive power they bring to you.

Think Positive Thoughts

These are not only your happy thoughts, but also the confident, powerful thoughts built through long hours of preparation. If you can think of no other positive thought, then use this one:

If you were asked to speak, somebody thought you were an expert in what you knew. If you asked to speak, YOU thought you were an expert in what you do. Either way, YOU are the expert. Your audience is privileged to hear from YOU!

Enjoy the Moment

This is the moment you stressed over, trained for, and will celebrate from. It's your moment in the spotlight, perhaps your "15 minutes of fame." Make the most of it – you'll always think back to this time as one of the great moments in your life!

What Happens Now?

If you've done your preparation, know your materials, and are mentally and physically ready, then only one thing CAN happen:

"I'm sitting in the front row, nervously awaiting my turn at the podium. The nervousness though is focused – I'm prepared and I'm ready! I was asked to present in front of this group because I'm an expert in my field. Nobody else knows the subject, they always come to me with questions. My notes are carefully prepared, but I won't even need them, for I have rehearsed this presentation a hundred times over. There's no need to worry about the PowerPoint® slides, I don't have any. My audience wants to hear from me, not a fancy animated word display.

I'm now being introduced. The audience applauds. I make my way to the podium, confidently lay my notes down, and deliver my well-rehearsed opening line. My voice is strong and confident. There is no quivering, no throat clearing, no "ums." The audience is in my hand. They are putty before me. I'm shaping them with my every word. Each of my points is clear, my illustrations vivid. I make eye contact with all of them. Forget that nonsense about seeing them in their underwear, I see their eyes.

The time passes so quickly up here. I begin to wind down and deliver a powerful conclusion. The audience stands and applauds. The questions and answer period now begins. My audience (yes, they are mine – I molded them with my words) has obviously listened to learn. They ask me questions that appear to be unanswerable to them, but the answers roll off my tongue. Heads nod in approval, and copious notes are taken. I'm the expert and they appreciate my sharing a few moments with them.

Alas, the time is up. Once again I hear thunderous applause. I quickly and gracefully move off the stage and out the back door. It was an incredible experience!"

A positive, life-changing event just occurred! You are a success. You'll forever be known as "that great speaker we had at the meeting last year." Life will be different for you now. People will ask you to help them prepare their presentation. You'll be asked for help developing visuals. People will want you to critique them. Novice presenters will want you to coach them.

Your schedule will become much busier. People need subject matter experts, particularly those that communicate well. Who knows, maybe you'll write books and give seminars? The world becomes full of exciting and wonderful opportunities when you master the art of public speaking!

Points to Ponder

1. Did I prepare as much as possible?

2. Am I physically ready to present?

3. Am I mentally ready to present?

4. Did I pack my materials carefully?

5. Am I ready for the new, exciting, and busy life I'll have after this successful presentation?

Chapter 5
Final Thoughts

There are a few more areas to cover before we conclude. The first area is that dreaded question and answer period after a presentation.

"Are there any questions?"

Why do we fear this event? Probably because no amount of preparation can give you every answer to every question. Even accomplished presenters, experts in their fields can get stumped by a question. Here are some suggestions to get you through a "Q and A" session unscathed.

Qualify Yourself

When you qualify yourself to an audience, you set the expectation for the Q and A session. Do this during your introduction. Take a look at the following example:

"Good evening. I'm Mack Munro and for the next 30 minutes, I'll be sharing some ideas with you about effective public speaking. Some of this will be new to you, and some will be a rehash of what you already know. Undoubtedly, there will be some great questions that we'll save for the end and I'll attempt to answer them. I can't promise I'll know all the answers, but I'll do my best and maybe we can all learn something new together."

So what did I tell the audience?

- I would share some ideas
- Some will be new
- Some you already know
- I know you'll have questions
- There will be a proper time to ask the questions
- I may not know the answer to your questions

Because I don't know the answer doesn't mean I didn't prepare. But at least they know that I'm in a learning mode, and in that mode, any answers I don't know are just new opportunities for all of us to learn. This way, the audience comes away feeling as if they were important too.

Acknowledge All Questions

"That's a great question."

This phrase is short but powerful. It does two things for you. First, it buys you a little time if you really don't know the answer. Second, it lets the audience know you appreciate their questions, even the tough ones.

I've discovered that it doesn't take much to get an audience on the defense, and like a cornered rattlesnake, they'll quickly mount an offense to confront you. We'll cover how to handle a hostile audience in a moment, but the best way to prevent it is to acknowledge the question and the asker. Make your audience feel important and they'll be less likely to turn on you. It's hard to beat up someone you like, and if your audience likes you, they'll be easier on you if you can't answer the question.

Think Before You Speak

When we get nervous, the temptation is to speak faster. Faster speech shortens the time to think, and so before you know it, you've said something you may regret.

When Arnold Schwarzenegger ran for Governor of California in 2003, he seemed a little surprised at the tenacity of reporters at press conferences. At one of his first appearances, during a flurry of questions, he was asked his opinion on gay marriage.

"I think that gay marriage is something that should be between a man and a woman," he answered.

Of course this answer was the only part of the interview seen by the public, but it's an example of speaking before thinking, which often happens (as in Arnold's case) when the question come quickly.

Don't be afraid to pause before answering. If you look like you have to think a moment, your audience will feel good because they'll think they're pretty intellectual. You'll give the impression the audience is important and you're giving them the best answer you can.

Don't Answer It If You Don't Know It

You don't have to know all the answers! If fact, your credibility will be higher if you admit you don't know it. After all, who knows everything? If indeed you knew everything, your audience would have no reason to come back and hear you speak again. Successful people are constant learners. Constant learners will admit they don't know anything.

If you don't know the answer, or are not at liberty to give it, be careful how you respond. Take a look at the following interesting response from Secretary of Defense Donald Rumsfeld given at a press conference in 2002:

"Reports that say something hasn't happened are always interesting to me, because as we know, there are known knowns; there are things we know we know.

We also know there are known unknowns; that is to say we know there are some things we do not know. But there are also unknown unknowns -- the ones we don't know we don't know."

I'm not exactly sure what he meant, but the answer leaves me even more curious. If you can't answer it, then don't. And please don't give a false or wrong answer! Giving a wrong answer instantly destroys your credibility. Insisting your wrong answer is correct ensures your credibility is destroyed for good.

Prepare a System To Get The Answers To Your Audience

It's always helpful to have a system in place to get difficult questions answered. Usually, I'll tell my audience in the beginning to write their questions down on the back of their business card and hand it to me as they leave and I'll get back to them. I also keep a stack of 3x5 cards with me and keep them available for those who don't have a business card.

Another system I like to use is the Parking Lot. This is usually a flip chart that I write the questions down on if they don't pertain to what we're talking about at the time. I can answer them later during the presentation, or at the end.

Develop a system that works for you. Thinking about what to do with the tough questions beforehand will give you extra confidence when you get them.

Calm a Hostile Audience

Audiences can be very fickle. There are some people that want to simply hear the sound of their own voice and steal the spotlight from you. And of course, there are just some people who want to be difficult. An audience can love you from start to finish or just until you hit one of their hot buttons. It's possible for mob behavior to happen if you let things get too far out of hand. Always have a plan in place to quell them if they start to get out of hand.

Know When To Say "Enough"

Remember, you are in charge of your presentation and your audience. It's ok to love your audience, but be prepared to corral them in if you have to. Establish some ground rules in the beginning if you know the topic is controversial – set the expectation to work in your favor. As in dealing with groups of children, it's easier to do it early before things get out of control.

When you feel the tension in the room beginning to rise, steer your presentation in a different direction. It can be subtle or overt, but make an effort to move forward or laterally. You can always come back to the point later when the tension dies down.

Don't Let The Audience Smell Blood

If a topic is controversial, which can make you appear controversial, expect there to be tension. Keep an eye on the tension. If you start to get flustered, the audience will see it. If they start rattling you and you begin to show any anger towards them, either verbally or non-verbally, they'll pick up on it. The once gracious audience will then band together and feed on you like hungry sharks.

When things get to this point, it's difficult to recover – and while you can, you'll probably lose any credibility you initially had. Keep a cool head, change the subject, move from your position in the front of the room, or reach for a lifeline.

Reach For A Lifeline

A lifeline is someone else in the room that has your back. It could be your co-facilitator if you have one, or someone else you designate. Your lifeline should be in an area at least 10 feet away from you. Their job is to divert the attention from you, long enough for you to gather yourself together and break the tension. Think about how the sound of a gunshot scatters a mob. Your lifeline should be able to stand and say something like:

"Wow, sounds like a controversial subject. I think what Mack is trying to say is...."

This shifts your audience's eyes and posture away from you. Use those few precious seconds to regroup. Then, get the audience back:

"Thanks Diane for that information. I'm sure the audience appreciates having two perspectives on this issue. Now let's take a look

at Point Number Four – and if time permits, we'll come back to Point Number Three."

Be sure to establish a signal with your lifeline beforehand and use it!

If you spend some time planning how to handle that Q and A session, it will go smoothly. If you master your subject, ultimately you'll probably look forward to it. There is a real satisfaction that comes from being in front of a group of people that want to hear from you, to draw from your knowledge, and to have you help them solve their problems.

One way to become an expert on any subject is to read about it at least one hour per day. Spend your time mastering your subject. If you can answer at least 75% of the questions confidently, you'll certainly be excused if you don't know the other 25%

Points to Ponder

1. Am I confident enough to answer random questions from your audience?

2. Do I have a "lifeline" I can trust to accompany me to my next presentation?

3. What steps can I take to become an expert in my subject?

We all want to have a successful presentation. It should be something we celebrate, and our audience remembers. But an unwelcome guest, Mr. Murphy, can always find a seat in your audience. We've spent most of this book talking about ways to work around him. But for the adventuresome folks reading this book, here are **six sure-fire ways to ensure he has a front row seat!**

Treating All Audiences The Same

We covered this in detail earlier in the book. Your audience is made up of unique individuals who share different values, attitudes, motivations, learning styles, personality preferences, ethnic backgrounds, language comprehension, intellectual abilities and experiences. They also may be experiencing illness, hunger, bad moods, stress, headaches, and boredom. Of course this is before you introduce your topic, which may be welcome to some and inflammatory to others.

Based on all this, why would you think a one-dimensional approach would work? Take some time and find out what you can about the audience, then tailor your approach to fit them.

Over-Reliance On Your Visuals (Particularly PowerPoint®)

We spent enough time on this one, but remember: YOU are who the audience came to see, not your slideshow. Use YOUR creativity, style and personality to get the information out. Visuals are just one of many tools you can use to do this.

Plan out your presentation, and then decide on the visuals. Develop at least one backup plan in case you face technical difficulties. If your visuals develop a glitch on stage, gracefully shift into Plan B. You'll come across as a true expert, knowledgeable, and cool under pressure. Fumbling around and looking helpless as your PowerPoint® slides malfunction will do nothing to build your credibility or hammer home your message.

Jokes

I know we covered this earlier, but the more confident you get, the more apt you are to experiment with new techniques. Don't get cute! If you have a sense of humor, use it subtly, naturally, and sparingly throughout the presentation. If you don't have a sense of humor, telling a joke won't make up for it. You risk offending people with a joke. No matter what the joke is, no matter if it deals with animals, vegetables, people, things, situations, cars, boats, cities, states, countries, fictitious characters, or even yourself, there is the inherent risk of offending someone.

Let your subject and your own natural personality win the audience. Funny people are born that way, humor comes naturally to them. Your gifts may be different, but everyone has them. Maximize your own strengths rather than borrow someone else's. Besides, just a smile is enough to make the audience like you. We all can learn to smile more often!

Talking Down To The Audience

Is your presentation designed to discipline or punish the audience? If not, be sure your tone, body language, or gestures won't do it for you.

An audience wants to feel appreciated and acknowledged positively. Presenters who talk down to audiences are rewarded with either open hostility, or passive-aggressive silence. Avoid finger pointing. If you must gesture, use an open hand, or the famous Disney two-finger point. Smile and keep your tone light and friendly. Let your audience know they're important and YOU are privileged to speak to them. Cherish their input and experience.

Answer their questions gladly and make them feel as though it's the first time you've ever heard that question, even if it's asked every time you speak. Understand that the Activist and Reflective learners are paying attention, just in a different way, so don't call them out or ridicule them if they appear to be disinterested. Love your audience and they'll love you back.

Annoyances ("um," "ya know," and "you guys")

Aside from making you look unpolished, annoyances (or filler words) could irritate your audience. *"Um"* and *"ya know"* do nothing more than distract, and even if you don't realize you're using them, the audience will. Practice will break you of this habit. Start working on it now before *"um"* and *"ya know"* become concrete in your vocabulary.

Many years ago when I was presenting while in the Navy, a female officer stood up and said, *"Excuse me, I am NOT a guy."* I was floored! It took me a second to realize what I said. I was using "you guys" when addressing the group. Now, if you look in the dictionary, you'll see that "you guys" is a recognized form of addressing a mixed gender audience. However, I've heard it used to address groups of children as well. Regardless of the group, or the appropriateness, don't use it! You'll sound unprofessional and could always risk having a female audience member take offense. Imagine if a mixed gender group was addressed as "you gals!"

Letting The Crowd Get Out Of Control

We covered this thoroughly in the Q and A section, but keep it in mind as you move through your presentation. Look for signs of restlessness or boredom in the audience. Listen carefully to the tone of the questions. Assess your materials, delivery, and pace constantly as you watch them.

If the crowd gets vocal, both verbally and non-verbally, use your lifeline, shift your subject, move around, or do anything reasonable to bring them back. Remember the gunshot effect on a mob. Keep a few tricks up your sleeve to gently but firmly get the audience back in your grasp.

Remember, presentations take work. Focus on perfection and you can't help but attain excellence. Avoid these six roadblocks and practice the following eight recipes for success.

Let's finish up with eight strategies to ensure you deliver that knockout! Most of this is all review, so we'll move through it quickly.

Control The Crowd

Lest we beat the proverbial dead horse any longer, remember this: You control a crowd only if you know them. When you know them, you can tailor a presentation to them. When you know them, you'll figure out when you're about to lose them, and when you can keep them, you'll positively impact them. Know your audience!

Have A Strong Introduction

Tell them what you'll be telling them. Do it in a way that engages them and intrigues them. A short story, quotation, or shocking statement works well. Let them know how long you'll be up there in front of them. Tell them what they should be learning from your presentation. The introduction introduces the journey – people like to know where you'll take them.

Be Informative

You were asked to speak because you're an expert in what you do. Your audience wants to learn from you so don't disappoint them. Be sure your presentation contains all the information necessary to inform. Outline it logically and pragmatically. Stick to the outline, but be flexible if you need to shift away to further inform. Make it your goal to teach at least one new thing to everyone in the audience.

Use Persuasive Strategies

Refer back in this book for these strategies, but remember, the purpose of a persuasive presentation is to mobilize your audience and move them forward. You can use this strategy for even informative or teaching presentations.

If you can mobilize and move an audience, you're doing the same thing that motivational speakers like Tony Robbins and Brendan Burchard do – perhaps a new career opportunity awaits you!

Maximize Your Credibility

Once again, you are an expert, otherwise you'd be in the audience, not in front of it. Use preparation as your springboard to maximizing your credibility. Don't rattle off your achievements or be a name-dropper. People can read all that stuff in your bio. Talk about what you know and what you do. Your knowledge and actions will exalt you more than your accolades and achievements. Inform and acknowledge your audience and you'll have more than enough credibility with them.

Use Verbal Support

Keep in mind the different personalities and learning styles of the audience. Be sure your examples and stories fit the broad range of people you'll have out there. Tie the unfamiliar to the familiar. Toggle your verbal support between the pragmatists and the theorists and you should reach everyone.

Use Visuals (Carefully)

Use the visuals, don't let them use you. Keep them clear, practical, and simple. Don't let the visuals upstage you. Use them only to solidify your points.

Have A Strong Conclusion

The conclusion wraps up everything you've said in a neat little package. It hammers home the main points and motivates the audience to move forward. It lets them know it's time to applaud. The introduction tells them what you'll be telling them. The body gives them the information, and the conclusion ties it together. All parts are important, but human beings like closure. Be sure to make a clear endpoint through a strong conclusion.

...and in conclusion:

Speaking in front of groups doesn't come naturally for everyone. We all get nervous, experience panic and a sense of unpreparedness.

However we can choose to break free from the fear and leverage the adrenaline. Good preparation, practice, positive visualization, expertise, self-knowledge, and still more practice will make you a confident presenter.

Surround yourself with positive people and creative thinkers. Join a support system like your local Toastmasters chapter. Volunteer to present often. Read one hour per day on subjects in your field of expertise. Practice your body language, gestures, voice tone, and smile. Watch other speakers and learn from them. Most of all, refuse to become a prisoner of your fear. Combine the techniques in this book with meticulous preparation and a positive attitude, and you will deliver a knockout presentation!

A Final Note for Those of You Who Are "The Boss"

If you're finished this book, you might be tempted to dismiss it since most was devoted to giving keynote talks. Trust me, if you want to be a great Boss, you really need to be a great speaker. If you visualize presenting in front of a huge audience, it will be much easier briefing your team of five each morning. If you imagine yourself giving a talk to hostile shareholders, think about how confident you'll be when you make a pitch to your own Boss.

Give yourself the gift of confidence and skill presenting in front of a group. You'll be glad you did.

"You gain strength, courage, and confidence by every experience in which you really stop to look fear in the face. You are able to say to yourself, 'I lived through this horror. I can take the next thing that comes along."

Eleanor Roosevelt

About the Author

Mack Munro is Founder and CEO of **Boss Builders** and is an experienced speaker, author, and practitioner who has worked with executive and management teams in companies of all types, sizes, and industries. He is the author of *How to Be a Great Boss, How to Build Better Bosses,* and several other business books.

He holds a Master of Arts degree in Organizational Leadership from Chapman University and a Bachelor of Science degree in Health Care Management from Southern Illinois University He is a qualified facilitator of the Myers-Briggs Type Indicator® and has also written and developed a number of personality and behavioral assessments and online tools.

Mack's background is primarily in Healthcare, Manufacturing, Consulting, Information Technology, Entrepreneurship, Leadership & Management, and Marketing. His typical clients come from these areas.

Prior to starting his company, Mack created training and professional development programs at U.T. Medical Group, Inc. in Memphis, TN, Holy Cross Hospital in Silver Spring, MD, and Contract Services Association of America in Arlington, VA. Mack has been an adjunct Professor of Business and Management at Vincennes University in Bremerton, WA and Crichton College in Memphis, TN. He a retired

United States Navy dental technician who served tours in Australia, Guam, Long Beach, California, and Bremerton, Washington.

Mack has been featured on radio, TV, and in print. He hosts the very popular podcast **The Boss Builder Podcast** where he provides information for newly-promoted supervisors, those who are in the role and are struggling, and even employees who are thinking about one day making the transition to management. He also hosts **HR Oxygen**, a podcast for the overworked, overstressed, overwhelmed, and under-appreciated HR Professional.

Mack can be reached at his corporate site:

TheBossBuilders.com

...and you can book him to speak at your event by visiting his speaking site:

MackMunro.com